PAPAS WITH
Ponytails

Alexandra Flowers

Copyright © 2019 Alexandra Flowers.

All rights reserved. No part of this book may be reproduced, stored, or transmitted by any means—whether auditory, graphic, mechanical, or electronic—without written permission of the author, except in the case of brief excerpts used in critical articles and reviews. Unauthorized reproduction of any part of this work is illegal and is punishable by law.

ISBN: 978-1-6847-1038-6 (sc)
ISBN: 978-1-6847-1037-9 (e)

Library of Congress Control Number: 2019914140

Because of the dynamic nature of the Internet, any web addresses or links contained in this book may have changed since publication and may no longer be valid. The views expressed in this work are solely those of the author and do not necessarily reflect the views of the publisher, and the publisher hereby disclaims any responsibility for them.

Any people depicted in stock imagery provided by Getty Images are models, and such images are being used for illustrative purposes only.
Certain stock imagery © Getty Images.

Artists Name For Cover Image Credit:
Lahna Brown, Bri Bare, and Victoria Gould

Lulu Publishing Services rev. date: 09/24/2019

DEDICATED TO

MY LOVING MOTHER

For images and more information about this book, please visit
PAPASWITHPONYTAILS.com

ACKNOWLEDGEMENTS

I wish to give special thanks to the following:

My children and their families for being such wonderful people

My partner, who put up with me while I wrote this book

My friends for their undying support and encouragement

All my amazing former students!

& to Spice for helping me figure out what is being affected in me

Disclaimer:
I have chosen to follow the tradition of anonymity with Alcoholics Anonymous by not using my real name as author of this book. At the request of my publisher I have also avoided using the full name of others mentioned in the book unless they are a celebrity or are listed in a citation. I struggled with using alternative names, but ultimately, I chose to change names rather than change my story. The stories and experiences I have shared within this book are true and factual from my point of view and are as I remember them.

PAPAS WITH PONYTAILS
By Alexandra Flowers

January 1980

At about 1:00 am, the phone rang next to my parents' bed. It was Ali asking for me. My parents called me into their room. I heaved my huge, pregnant body up out of the bed and rushed to the phone. He told me he was in London waiting for a flight to Iran. All I really remember from the call was hearing my traumatized little two-year-old crying "Mommy" on the other end. My world began to spin, and I collapsed to the floor in despair. My son was gone! I had never been so horrified! I don't remember much after that...

CONTENTS

Chapter 1	Trauma	1
	Iranian Hostage Crisis	3
	One More Try	5
Chapter 2	Dam Brat	9
	Shyness and Insecurity	9
	Lions	10
	Geographical Cure	10
	One-Room School	15
	Young Teen	16
	Eugene	18
	Three Times a Charm?	18
Chapter 3	Dangerous Mind	21
	California	22
	I Believed in Fairy Tales	23
Chapter 4	Luke	27
	My First Trips to Iran	29
	Cultural Differences	30
	Drug Smuggler	32
	College	33
	Surgery in The Third Trimester	35

Chapter 5	Leaving My Heart Behind	39
	The Church	41
	Little Lyle	44
	Kelly	47
	Brief Return of Luke	48
	Theo	49
Chapter 6	Costa Rica	51
	Foreign Language & Giant Bugs	51
	Costa Rican Food	53
	Speaking Spanish	55
	Climate	56
	Life in Costa Rica	58
	Palmita	59
	San Isidro del General	61
	Refugee Camp	63
	Transportation	66
	More Machine Guns!	68
	End of A Chapter	69
Chapter 7	Alcohol And Freedom From Religion	71
	Return to the States	71
	Custody Battle	74
	Another Chapter in My Life	76
	Cross Between Insanity & Salvation	77
	My First Grandchild	80
	Drugs	81
Chapter 8	Recovery	85
	Spice	86
	Higher Power	87
Chapter 9	Fulfilling A Life-Long Dream!	93
	Sunny	94
	Return of Lyle	95

	Joe.. 96
	College Life... 101
Chapter 10	Return To My Hometown... 105
	Haunted House... 107
	Living with My Parents 108
	Another Ghost!.. 108
	Dale 109
	My Parenting Style 112
Chapter 11	Papa 115
	Ralph 120
Chapter 12	Upward Bound... 123
	Working with Teens 123
	College Trips 127
	My Retirement 129
	My Health.. 131
Chapter 13	Luke's Return... 133
	Las Vegas Wedding 140
Chapter 14	My Family Today 143
	Bessie & Her Family 143
	My Boys.. 146
Chapter 15	The Last Of The Lions... 149
Bibliography... 153	

CHAPTER 1

Trauma

A few weeks after a divorce where I was awarded full legal custody of my son, Luke, and unborn child, and only days before the baby was born, I allowed Ali to go with me to a doctor appointment. He had offered to watch our two-year-old son while I was in the examining room. I was already more than two weeks past my due date. When I returned to the lobby, Ali and my baby boy weren't there. The receptionist said Ali had asked her to tell me that he was running an errand and would be right back. I went outside to wait for them. I remember it was a freezing cold day and there was a lot of snow on the ground. January in Wyoming can be harsh.

Remember, readers; this was the pre-cell phone era. I don't recall how long I stood outside waiting before finally gathering the courage to go back inside and ask to use the phone. I do remember the receptionist was surprised that I had still been outside waiting in the cold. Being as shy as I was, even the thought of going back inside the doctor's office to ask for help caused me anxiety.

I didn't know what else to do, so I called my mom. She left work to come pick me up. We went home and began calling everyone we could think of, including the hospital and police, to see if anyone had seen Ali and Luke or might know where they were. Around 10:00 pm we got a call from the sheriff's office that my car had been found at the airport. My first

thought was that Ali went to see an uncle of his in another state. I tried to call the uncle, but to no avail.

To say I was distraught was an understatement, but I didn't think that Ali would actually have taken Luke and left the country. I just couldn't believe he would do something that extreme. The next few hours were filled with tears and anguish. I finally managed to fall into a fitful sleep that night despite my turmoil, fear, and heartache. The unborn baby was over-due, and I was miserable. All I could think of was my little boy.

At about 1:00 a.m. the phone rang next to my parents' bed. It was Ali asking for me. My parents called me into their room. I heaved my huge, pregnant body up out of the bed and rushed to the phone. He told me he was in London waiting for a flight to Iran. All I really remember from the call was hearing my traumatized little two-year-old crying "Mommy" on the other end. My world began to spin, and I collapsed to the floor in despair. My son was gone! I had never been so horrified! I don't remember much after that.

The next day, my mom called my doctor to see if he could help ease my suffering, but as I recall, he seemed apathetic to my situation. The next few days were a tumultuous blur, filled with tears and anguish - mine, as well as my parents'.

Five days later I went into labor, and within six hours I had delivered a healthy eight-pound baby girl. Bessie was born with big, beautiful brown eyes and dark hair that reached down to her shoulders. She was so precious, and my parents were such a tremendous help! We all fell in love with her instantly. I adored my new little girl, and did my best to be a good mommy, but I was still devastated. I wanted Luke. I can't imagine how I would have survived without my parents. I was breast-feeding and nurturing my baby, but I was heartbroken.

Ali hadn't waited for Bessie to be born since I had assured him the baby was a girl. They had a saying in Iran that "you love a son as soon as he is born, and you learn to love a daughter." I recall one of the times I had visited Iran previously, when relatives had given birth to a baby girl. It was their second daughter, and instead of celebrating her healthy birth, everyone was mourning because she wasn't a boy.

In my desolation, I felt I couldn't live without my son. Having my new baby girl helped, but my days were filled with anguish and despondency. It

was easy to forget the abuse and suffering of my marriage when all I could think of was the longing for my son. Within a couple months, I began to plot to go to Iran to get him back. Ali was thrilled when he called me one day and I told him I would come back to him. He confessed to me that he only took Luke to get even with me for leaving him.

I still feared and hated the man, of course, but I was willing to do anything to be with my precious son. I didn't even tell my poor parents what I was doing until the last minute out of fear they would try to stop me. I was blinded by emotion and despair. Ali procured a plane ticket for me, and I easily added Bessie to my passport.

I'm ashamed to admit this now, but when I went shopping at the local department store a few days before I left the country to buy baby clothes and a few things I thought I would need, I wrote a bad check. My thought was that I would be out of the country and it wouldn't matter. I found out much later, that my mom covered that check. It was only around a hundred dollars, and she says now that she doesn't even remember doing it. However, I am remorseful to this day. I was such a mess emotionally.

Thank you, Mom. I'm so sorry for the pain I caused you and Dad. You went through this crisis too. You lost your only grandson, and then I took your precious granddaughter. I was so selfish in my actions, but I was blinded by my desperation.

I left with my three-month-old daughter and somehow made it to Iran. I don't remember many details of what all I did to get there, but Ali was waiting for me at the airport when I arrived. He was thrilled to see us. I was exhilarated to see Luke, and Luke was so happy to be with his loving mommy again. Our reunion was intense. I should note that there was much political turbulence going on between Iran and the United States at this time.

Iranian Hostage Crisis

Back in November of 1979, when I was nearly eight months pregnant, Iranian revolutionaries invaded the U.S. embassy in Tehran, the capitol city of Iran, and took more than sixty American embassy employees as hostages.

Mostly students, these revolutionaries were rebelling against the United States for allowing the formerly exiled shah of Iran into the United States for cancer treatment. Reports indicate that the takeover was actually more about breaking ties with historical American interference in Iranian government affairs.

Tensions between Iran and the United States had gone on for years. Mohammed Reza Pahlavi, the shah of Iran, had been working with Americans when it came to oil and foreign aid, but he was considered a brutal dictator who tortured and murdered thousands of his people. Under the reign of the shah, the Iranian government spent millions on American-made weapons while the Iranian economy suffered.

By the late 1970's, Islamic revolutionaries had taken over the country and exiled the shah from Iran. Their new government was led by Ayatollah Khomeini, a radical Islamic cleric. The ayatollah installed a militant Islamist government and cut ties with the United States. The embassy hostages were held captive for more than a year: 444 days to be exact. There are many articles to be found today discussing the nightmare they went through (*Iran Hostage Crisis*).

I remember hearing about the embassy takeover when it first happened, and I recall Ali being concerned about how it might affect his presence in the United States. I didn't really have much understanding of it at the time, though, and never dreamed it would become a part of my own history in some way. I ended up traveling to Iran to find Luke just a few months after the embassy was seized and the employees there were captured.

There were times while I was in Iran that some of the hostages were shown on the news. I didn't know the purpose for them being televised, because I couldn't understand the language, but they were blindfolded and looked terrified. I recognized their fear and anxiety.

Not long after I arrived in Iran, President Jimmy Carter launched a rescue operation, attempting to send an elite military team to the embassy. Tragically, a severe sandstorm caused several helicopters to malfunction. Eight American soldiers were killed, and the mission was aborted. Of course, I knew very little about what was actually happening at the time. While in Iran myself, I was only told that the Iranian people were celebrating a failed rescue attempt by the Americans.

Sadly, my own personal nightmare took precedence over political

matters in my anguished mind. However, my own eventual escape from Iran was expedited when President Carter offered promissory notes to all Americans wishing to leave the country. There is much history I am leaving out, but this is the information that I understood at the time.

One More Try

Resuming the story of my return to Iran, Ali's family was delighted to see me and were thrilled to meet little Bessie. The four of us shared a room in his parents' home and I pretended to be married to him again even though we were legally divorced. I thought I could live for my son. I tried to be a good wife. I already knew how to walk on eggshells around Ali and to be careful not to make him angry, but even that is difficult when the person is emotionally unstable.

I had met his family twice before, and I loved his mom. She was always tender and loving toward me. I wrote lots of letters to my parents, but Ali always reviewed and approved them before I was allowed to mail them. I was careful not to say anything negative or admit there were any problems. I was treated like a prisoner. I wasn't allowed to leave the house without him or a family member and had no friends. Ali exerted complete control over everything I did, and I experienced much fear on a daily basis at his hands. I don't mean to undermine the suffering that the true embassy hostages endured, but I felt like I was a hostage, too.

I did try to maintain a positive attitude. I was kind to all his extended family members (the female ones), and I put much effort into trying to learn Farsi. I have since learned that I have a gift for languages, and I did pick up quite a few words, although I have forgotten most of them by now. His family was good to me and I was happy to have my children, but I was still living with a man I feared and despised. I tried, though. At one point I decided that if he remarried me, I would devote myself to trying to be a good wife and mother. When I asked him if we could get remarried, he refused. That is when I found out that Ali had not told his family we were divorced.

One time, when we were visiting Tehran, we drove past the U.S. embassy that was under siege. I have always been blonde and did not cover

up because Ali didn't allow me to, even though concealing the head and most of the body is the culturally correct behavior for a woman there; especially with the religious sector having taken over the country. It was obvious to all that I was American. My memory is like slow motion as I remember the Iranian guards watching and pointing their machine guns at me while we drove past the embassy. I can still sense the incredulity and disbelief that I felt.

Another time, when I was walking near the house with my sister-in-law, a man on a motorcycle rode past. He slowed down as he drove by us, and he reached out and struck me in the shoulder with his fist. I do know what it feels like to be treated as an unwelcome minority.

Occasionally, when I was especially homesick, Ali would allow me to call my parents. The phone system was quite different there. They did not receive itemized phone bills. In fact, on the patio outside the house, there was a small box on the wall with a switch that had to be turned on before long-distance or overseas calls could be made from any phones within the three apartments of the house. The box was kept locked and Ali's parents kept the key on a hook in their bedroom.

On the rare occasions that I was allowed to call home, Ali would always be right there listening to everything I said and making sure I didn't say anything he did not want me to say. I was carefully supervised and controlled.

Although I enjoyed learning more about the culture, and even met a couple other American women who were married to Iranian men, I was still very unhappy in my relationship. I loved my babies, but things were getting worse with Ali. I felt he was awful to his mother, too. To me, she was a saint. Even though we didn't speak the same language, we seemed to have a strong connection. Maybe it was something like a victims' bond. She was yelled at a lot for petty things and seemed to be treated as badly as I was. It seemed to me that she was frequently trying to hide her tears. Of course, I didn't dare say a word for fear of the repercussions. I slowly began to realize more and more that I could no longer tolerate how I was living.

One day, when everyone else was gone and the children were napping, I took advantage of the opportunity and wrote a letter to my mom. I admitted how awful it really was and that all my letters and phone calls were monitored. It was a hastily written letter, and I gathered up the

babies and rushed to the mailbox down the street to mail it. After enough time had passed that I felt certain she got my letter, I began watching and waiting for the opportunity to call my mom without Ali around. Ali's parents always kept their bedroom door locked, but I knew that was where the key to the long-distance call box was held.

One day, the babies and I were the only ones at home with his mom, and she was preparing to leave. As she was locking her bedroom door, I made eye contact with her and gave her a questioning look. My eyes asked, "don't you trust me?" As I said, we seemed to have some sort of a mental connection. After she departed, I saw that she had left the key in the lock of the bedroom door! I didn't hesitate. I went into her room, took the key off the hook and headed to the balcony outside. I quickly opened the phone box on the wall. Flipping the long-distance switch, I ran back inside and called my mom. I knew that unless I got caught making the call, they would never know since they did not receive itemized phone bills.

Oh, the relief in finally being able to talk honestly to my mom in private! She had received my letter, and had, in fact, already set things in motion to help me get home! We had to talk quickly, but plans were made. She had contacted the state senator's office and they put her in touch with the United States State Department in Washington DC. Since there was no longer a functioning U.S. embassy in Iran due to the siege, plans were made via the Swiss Embassy in Tehran.

Mom told me that President Jimmy Carter had made an advisory that all Americans should leave Iran, and he made it possible for us to do so. The U.S. would provide promissory notes to all Americans wanting to leave the country to pay the airfare back to the states, which could be paid back at a later date. I don't remember all the details now, but we made plans for mom to call me back once it was set up, scheming to speak in veiled conversation if I was not alone when she called. I rushed to relock the phone box with feelings of hope and excitement and returned the key to its rightful place. Thankfully, I was successful, and did not get caught.

When Ali returned, I lied and told him Mom called me and wanted us to come for a vacation. Miracle of miracles; he consented! When she called me back with details, we convinced him it was just a visit, and he assumed Mom and Dad were paying for tickets for me and the kids.

The rest is a bit of a blur in my memory, but one of the things we had to

do was complete paperwork with Ali's signature, giving written permission for his wife and children to leave the country. Remember, he didn't tell anyone we were divorced, and women have no rights in Iran. I could not leave the country without his consent.

We traveled the 425 miles to Tehran and spent the night with an uncle. The morning we arrived at the airport Ali announced he would only let me leave with Bessie; Luke was to stay with him. I cannot begin to express the anguish I felt over this mandate. I loved little Luke with my entire being. I had dreamt of this child long before he was born. How could I leave him? I was mortified because I also knew without a doubt that I could no longer pretend to tolerate the emotional abuse and torment that Ali provided. I HAD to go. I was in anguish as I listened to my baby boy crying for me as I walked away. I told myself I would see him again. I told myself his grandma would take good care of him, that he would be loved and cherished. I promised myself we would be together again soon. I still get tears in my eyes and a lump in my throat just thinking about that fateful day. I got on the plane with my little Bessie, who was now 6 months old, and left my beloved son behind.

CHAPTER 2

Dam Brat

Shyness and Insecurity

Many times, people have wondered how individuals can make the choices in their lives that lead to them being in relationships with abusive and/or controlling partners. I can only speak for myself, but I have seen similar patterns in others.

For me, it was about shyness and insecurity.

I think I was put on this planet to learn to overcome fear. In my opinion, shyness is a symptom of fear. According to Healthline.com (*Heitz*) the definition for shyness is:

> "a feeling of fear or discomfort...shyness is an unpleasant feeling of self-consciousness — a fear of what other people are thinking. This fear can inhibit a person's ability to do or say what he wants. It can also prevent the healthy formation of healthy relationships. Shyness is often linked to low self-esteem. In its extreme form, it is considered social anxiety."

I definitely suffered from shyness; for as long as I can remember. I can personally relate to the expression "frozen with fear." This book isn't about

analyzing my fear and shyness, but rather to better understand how far I have come. When I was younger, I would "be" with just about anyone who would have me. I had the love of my family and parents, so I'm not blaming them for my insecurity. But I was always so afraid of saying or doing the wrong thing, I would frequently say or do nothing. I was highly over sensitive and "got my feelings hurt" way too easily.

You will see examples of my shyness and insecurity in various scenarios throughout this book. Although I have made many accomplishments that I am very proud of, I believe that overcoming fear has been the greatest achievement in my life. I still have concerns; don't get me wrong. But I have made huge strides in my life when it comes to conquering fear and insecurity. I am still uncomfortable going into an unfamiliar situation, but I force myself to do it anyway and it usually turns out fine. I want to share the progression of a recurring dream that I had over the years as an adult.

Lions

For many years, I experienced lions surrounding my dreams. When approaching the outskirts of my dreams, I would see these huge, intimidating lions. There were hundreds of them surrounding the borders of my dreams. They would always stop me in my tracks. I would experience fear and not go any further. I would simply turn around and go back to whatever I had been dreaming. These dreams continued for many years.

Geographical Cure

I was born in a small Nebraska town. I loved horses, and my mom tells me that one of my first words was "horsey." I learned to read by the time I was four years old, but I was so shy as a child that my parents were advised to start me in Kindergarten before I turned five. They were told it would help me overcome my shyness. (I don't think it worked.) I was always the youngest child in my class.

Papas with Ponytails

As a preteen I used to lament how boring my life was. Looking back, there was so much more to my life than I realized. We have all heard the term "military brat" to describe people whose family lived in many different places while their parent was in the military. We moved around a lot as I was growing up. So, I like to say I was a "dam brat" (as opposed to a "damn brat"). My dad worked for the United States Bureau of Reclamation as a power plant operator for various dams.

My Mom is a very caring and loving woman. She was the oldest of eight kids and had been a caretaker for as long as she can remember. Everyone who knows my mom loves her. While I always loved and adored my mom and considered myself fortunate to have her as my mother, I was very much a "daddy's girl."

My dad was an amazing man. He was fun-loving, handsome and charming. He was also a self-proclaimed alcoholic – not the sort who drank every day, but once he started drinking, he had trouble stopping. I could tell lots of stories about his stints of imbibing, but fortunately he was never violent, and his bouts were infrequent.

As a child, when my dad did drink, he always seemed fun to me, but my mom would get terribly upset. I often remember listening to her yell and cry after he came home late. I felt terrible for my mom's unhappiness, but I hated listening to the fighting so much that I vowed to myself at a very young age I would never be a screamer and/or yeller. I wanted to be more like my dad...

> *I went on to become an alcoholic myself. I won't go into the definition or debate over whether I was a REAL alcoholic, but my drinking did cause problems in my life, which led to eventual drug use. Learning to give up alcohol was vital for my survival. I also believe that my drug and alcohol use later in life could have been avoided had I sought counseling rather than chemicals to relieve my pain.*

My parents (I realize now) tried a geographical cure for my dad's drinking when I was ten years old. A geographical cure is when you think moving to a new place will help you change your behavior. My younger brother Ralph, eleven months my junior, was nine. Joe, my older brother,

was twelve. Our first big move was to an extremely small town. Mom and Dad both came from large families, so it was quite a change to leave all my grandparents, aunts, uncles, and cousins to go live practically in the middle of nowhere.

The town was located at the top of a mountain in central Wyoming. In fact, we were always told they blew the top off the mountain and built a government camp, and that's just how it appeared. There were several houses, a post office, a small community center, and a one room school house. The school was in one room with a small apartment on the side for the teacher who had transferred there from a larger town. She and her husband lived in the tiny apartment attached to the school. There were only a handful of students attending; in fact, I think six were the most students ever enrolled in the two years we lived there. We used to joke about the fact that when our family moved away, we took half the school with us.

The small settlement was surrounded by beautiful mountains and forest and was many miles away from any towns large enough to have stores. Going grocery shopping was an all-day process and the journey itself was treacherous in the mind of that ten-year-old girl. Driving along winding mountain roads was horrifying to me. The first few times I hid my head so that I couldn't see all the twists and turns on the narrow road which had steep mountains on one side and seemingly bottomless pits on the other. I was so frightened. It took months before I was able to relax while riding in the car on those roads. Of course, mountainous roads don't bother me at all today. There is a lesson there, too, in overcoming fear.

We had lots of animal visitations in our yard; deer, rabbits, etc. One of the most pronounced wildlife memories I have is of the mountain goats. I can still visualize my mom chasing them away with the broom so she could go hang clothes on the line. More than once, my dad had to help pull porcupine quills out of the shrieking neighbor dog's muzzle.

We didn't have a lot of money – but we somehow had plenty of food. We got pork from my grandpa who raised hogs, and to this day, I think a good pork roast is one of the best meats I have ever tasted. Of course, my mom was always an excellent cook. I did not appreciate it however, when she tried to expand the budget by serving us things like powdered milk. I loved milk as a child, and was not fooled by the nasty substitution, even

when she tried to mix it half and half with real milk. She was creative in stretching the food, though and we never went hungry.

Our family also hunted and ate lots of moose, elk, deer, antelope and rabbit. To this day, I am not fond of game meat. Because beef was such a rare treat growing up, I prefer it today. We always had a nice garden with lots of fresh produce during the summer and Mom would can fruits and vegetables and make pickles and jellies for us to eat throughout the year. I still do not like store-bought jelly.

I did have many great outdoor experiences living atop this mountain. We did plenty of fishing, hiking, learning to love nature, and so much more. I always felt sorry for the fish that were caught. My family still likes to make fun of me for "kissing the fish" when I was young as I mourned their deaths.

Hunting is another story. Dad taught me how to shoot a gun, and frankly, I was a very good shot. I wasn't old enough to hunt big game, but I could sure shoot a rabbit. In fact, for a while I had a reputation in that small community for being the best shot among the kids. That ended the day I shot a rabbit and only injured it.

I still remember that poor little bunny's screams and I have not been able to shoot another animal since. I do still eat meat, and understand hunting for food, but I can't bring myself to be the one who actually kills the animal. It may seem hypocritical, especially to a vegetarian or vegan, but I'm not ready to give up one of my favorite foods; meat. I believe that man was designed to be an omnivore. I do, however, abhor trophy hunting for prize mounts and glory.

Ralph and I were very close when we were little. Being just eleven months apart in age, we were often mistaken for twins. As kids, my favorite game with Ralph was when we would go down the side of the densely forested mountain and make-believe that we were little kids who were lost! It's funny to me now, considering we WERE little kids; pretending to be lost.

Those were the days when kids could go outside to play, and parents didn't have to worry about where they were. When Mom woke up early in the morning and we weren't in our beds, she would simply go to the side of the hill and call for us. Ralph and I played together all the time. When we weren't outside, he would play Barbies or troll dolls with me, or

we designed and built cardboard houses, and I would play cars with him. I still remember observing the adults sitting around watching us kids while we ran, jumped and played, and telling myself "I will never stop having lots of energy!" (*Oh, to be young, again!*)

> *I debated whether or not to put the following excerpt into my story, but the truth is; it happened, and it caused me distress for many years.*

There was a family living in the government camp with us who we were very close to. The couple was older, and had their grown son, who was probably in his late thirties, living with them. He was a heavy-set man in a wheelchair resulting from injuries he had suffered in an accident many years before we met them. He was great with all the kids and took a particular liking to me. He would take me hunting and gave me lots of attention and positive reinforcement.

My pleasure in being befriended by this man was short-lived, however. *I will refer to him as "Frank."* My "friendship" with Frank came to an end when he called me to him one day and proceeded to slip his hand into my pants and touch me inappropriately. I was mortified. I was completely frozen with fear. He told me not to tell anyone, and as a young girl, I had no idea what to do. I honestly cannot recall how often he touched me, but it was awful for me. I went out of my way to try and avoid him. The adults in my life were confused when I no longer wanted to go hunting with him or spend time with him.

One day, our family was at their house and Mom suggested I go upstairs and tell Frank something. I screamed, "No! I hate him!" I burst into tears and proceeded to run out of the house toward home. Of course, everyone had overheard me. Mom chased after me in anger for my disrespectful outburst. As I sobbed, I told her that I didn't like how he touched me. Mom seemed shocked but just warned me to never tell anyone.

Nothing about it was ever mentioned again, but at least I was no longer expected to be left alone with him. It always bothered me that I wasn't supposed to talk about it when it had such a powerful, negative impact on me. I relate this story because there are so many people who had similar experiences when they were young and were commanded to never talk

about it. I've always been ashamed to admit it, but years later when Mom told me Frank had died…I was happy to hear it.

One-Room School

Attending a one-room school was quite an experience. As I said previously, the teacher was an older woman who lived in the tiny adjoining apartment with her husband. I was the only student in the fourth and fifth grades and since I was a such a good, quiet little girl, I was mostly left to do my own studying and assignments. I still remember the teacher often giving me huge pages of division problems to do. I never cared for math and it didn't take me long to figure out that when she corrected my work, she did not refer to an answer sheet. She would have me stand at her desk beside her and she would go through each problem I had written down one by one, solving them as we went along. I quickly learned to pick six or seven problems and just redo each one in random order several times throughout the page. She never caught on.

I didn't really think of her as a nice person, although there are only two times I remember getting into trouble at school. Once was when the entire school body (there were only six of us) was reprimanded because none of us brought a birthday card for her husband on his birthday. I don't think any of us even knew it was his birthday, and we barely knew him, but I do remember she was very angry and yelled at us a lot. I never handled being yelled at very well and I still shut down when someone raises their voice at me.

The second time I recollect getting in trouble in school, was shortly before Christmas one year. She had brought a big stocking full of tiny gifts to the school and had a contest. Each student was to write down their name and guess the number of gifts in the stocking. The student with the nearest correct answer would win it. Ralph and I coincidentally guessed the same number. Since it was also the correct number, she accused us of cheating! She claimed we must have snuck into her apartment while she was sleeping and counted the number of items inside! I remember her being somewhat hysterical. Ralph and I were dumbfounded. We were only nine and ten years old and had not done any such thing. We didn't even know

the stocking existed until she brought it to class that day. We just got lucky, I guess. Lucky in guessing the correct number that is; our punishment was that neither of us won the stocking full of prizes. I think she gave it to the student who came closest after us. I was very hurt and disappointed. It's ironic how something so trivial still sticks in my mind. These are the little things a child never forgets.

This is also the same teacher who told me I looked terrible in red when I wore a pretty, new red dress to school one day. I never again wore red until I was an adult. Even then, I was uncomfortable in red for many years. My poor mom probably never understood why I stopped wanting to wear that red dress! I was definitely over-sensitive as a child, but I believed the words of that cruel teacher.

We lived in this small town for a couple years. When Joe was finishing the eighth grade, Mom and Dad were faced with the dilemma of where he would attend school the next year, since that school didn't have higher grades. Dad ended up applying for a job transfer, and we soon moved to another small Wyoming town.

Young Teen

Once again, we lived in government housing and Dad worked at the dam there. This community was much larger than the previous one but the population of the town today is less than 300 people, although I think it may have been more populated back in the late sixties when we were there. Many of the town's residents lived outside of the town as farmers and ranchers. Every dam has a lake, and the reservoir there was (and still is) very popular. During the summers, a multitude of tourists, fishermen and boat enthusiasts inundate the small town.

The school housed students in grades Kindergarten through twelfth. There hadn't been any girls my age in our previous community, but I did make a few friends in this town. I was still very shy and insecure, though. Starting a new school in junior high was difficult. I still feel like fourteen is the worst age to be as far as insecurity and emotions. I think I cried myself to sleep every night throughout puberty. Hormones, lack of confidence, shyness, and lots of tears were a major part of my life during

my adolescence. We lived in this town for four years; during most of my teen years.

Still overly sensitive, I remember being very hurt when classmates did things such as telling their parents they were spending the night with me, when I discovered they were actually going somewhere else. Looking back, I now realize they were sneaking away with boys, but at the time they lied to me and I took it very personally. I wallowed in my self-pity. I was one of those people who always thought everyone was talking ill about me or making fun of me. *(Today I have been known to say, "don't be so worried about what people are thinking of you…because they probably aren't").*

I was a huge fan of the Monkees at that time and several girls and I started a fan club. The Monkees were a TV show about four young men in a band. I remember all of us dreaming about marrying one of them. Trying to be realistic, I once suggested my beautiful aunt who lived in California should marry Davy Jones, my favorite Monkee. My friends then proceeded to hit, punch and kick me for suggesting such a thing. Of course, I was hurt more emotionally than physically.

When I was thirteen, I was given a Siamese kitten by my grandmother whose cat had a large litter. I named her Cleopatra. She was quite small and very loving. Since I cried myself to sleep most nights at that age, Cleo became my consoler. Whenever I wept, she would come curl up near my face and cuddle me until I finally drifted off to sleep. She gave me so much comfort throughout my adolescence and I have many tender memories of her.

My parents were very over-protective of me and I was not allowed to go out at night unless I had a good excuse. I remember signing up for an after-school music class just so I could leave the house those evenings. It probably wouldn't have mattered to me so much if they'd had the same rules for my brothers.

Gender guidelines were a big deal back then. Household chores were done by Mom and I and outdoor responsibilities were completed by Dad and my brothers. While Mom did make my brothers help with the dishes once in a while, Dad would never allow me to do things like mow the lawn. If fact, I never learned to enjoy football. When "the guys" sat around watching the sport on television, I was expected to help Mom with

cooking, cleaning, and even serving the guys who were just sitting around watching television. I grew up resenting the game.

I will never forget the year I begged my parents for a guitar for Christmas. They didn't have a lot of money, so when the opportunity arose to purchase a used electric guitar and amplifier from my uncle, my parents jumped on it. What could have brought great joy, turned out to be heartbreaking for me. Why? They gave the guitar to my big brother who had never asked for one because it seemed like a "boy" gift, rather than a "girl" gift.

Eugene

When I was about thirteen and my cute little cousin Gene was eight years old, he came to live with us. His mother, one of my mom's sisters, was having major surgery. She was the single mom of three children living in California and the three kids were divided up among relatives while she recuperated. I was thrilled to have Gene living with us and still think of him more as a brother than a cousin. He ended up living with us for the next eight years. I have many fond memories of doing things with Gene as we grew up. He frequently helped me with dishes, and we had many bonding discussions over the sink. We are still close today and he shares the basement of my home.

Three Times a Charm?

Dad did well with staying away from alcohol when we first moved to this town, but eventually he began drinking once more. The cycle of Dad coming home late, and listening to Mom yelling and crying continued. It may have been a small town, but it still had a couple bars and Dad was very popular and social. By the time I was in high school, my parents once more attempted a geographical cure and we moved yet again. I was excited about the move this time; looking forward to a fresh start in a new place. I suppose I thought people might like me better if they didn't really know me.

Mom and Dad tried the geographical cure for the third time when we moved to a little town in Utah and Dad transferred to work at the dam there. It was another extremely small town but had nice, brick government housing that we lived in. It was a beautiful place and I have many fond memories of it. The earth around the reservoir is filled with rich, red tones and surrounded by a lush national forest My first summer job (other than babysitting) was as a dishwasher at a lodge and restaurant there. Once again, there were many tourists visiting during the summer as the lake and surrounding areas are gorgeous.

There was a small elementary school that Gene attended and Ralph, Joe and I rode the bus through dense forest about an hour each way to attend high school. We saw a lot of moose and other forest animals on that daily trip. I was still terribly shy and insecure during high school, but I loved theater. I could become someone else when I had a role in a play, so I performed every chance I got. Sadly, it was a small town so there weren't many opportunities.

I did make a few friends there but didn't get very close with anyone. I tried joining the other kids in all their wild activities. I recall when several of us would load up in a car at school lunchtime and go smoke cigarettes. I came back puking my guts out. Needless to say, I have never been a smoker and cigarettes still make me sick. I also remember riding in the back seat of the car with my pretty friends and looking at myself in the rear-view mirror. "Man, I'm ugly," I would tell myself.

I had one friend whose parents owned a ranch nearby. Many weekends were spent at her ranch. I still love horses and had many opportunities to ride with her. Besides horse-back riding, I got to participate in moving cattle, brandings, and witnessing the birth of animals. One time a cow dropped her calf (gave birth) while the herd was being moved from winter pasture to summer fields. Due to the stress of moving, she abandoned it. My friend and I cleaned the afterbirth from the little calf and she suckled my fingers as we returned her to the ranch. We named her Luv and bottle-fed her. I still remember seeing her after she was a mama cow herself. Her calf wouldn't come near us, but Luv would come right up for hugs and affection.

The summer before my senior year of high school, when I was sixteen, I flew in an airplane for the first time. I flew to Chicago to visit an aunt and uncle who lived there. It was an amazing summer. I met many new people and had lots of new, exciting experiences They had a very large, beautiful old home. I recall my aunt introducing me to their roommate who rented one of their rooms. A few days after meeting her, my aunt asked me what I thought of her. She seemed like a nice woman but I hadn't given her much thought. My aunt then asked if it bothered me that she was black. I was dumbfounded. I hadn't even noticed. Everyone has different colored skin, hair, eyes, etc. It just goes to show, that racism is learned behavior.

While I was in Chicago that summer, I was contacted with the news that there was a school yearbook meeting. I had been selected as the editor of the school paper before the semester had ended. Rather than wait until my return, I was informed they were giving the position to another (very popular) girl because she was there and I wasn't. I sometimes wonder how that may have changed my future, but I don't regret my time in Chicago.

I finished high school when I was 17 and barely remember my high school graduation. Since I was expected to ride home after the ceremony with my parents, I shared a bottle of cheap wine with a fellow graduate whose older brother had given us a ride to the school beforehand. I was pretty tipsy standing in front of everyone during the ceremony, and by the time the family went out for a nice celebratory dinner and I rode home with them afterwards, I was ready for bed! Those are my only memories of my high school graduation.

Shortly after graduating high school, I decided I was going to take a huge step in my life and move to California.

CHAPTER 3

Dangerous Mind

In my experience, the mind is a dangerous place to be. I learned years ago that I have what I now call a magical magnifying mind; I cannot always trust what I am thinking and telling myself. Today, I know it is important - no, imperative - that I try to fill my mind with positive, productive thoughts. I used to let my imagination go wild. An active imagination is great, but not if I am imagining negative things. For me it is dangerous to let my mind run amok with possible scenarios, imagined conversations, and so much more.

The worst was when I would begin to feel sorry for myself. The negative thoughts could go on endlessly, leading to insecurity, self-loathing, fear, sadness, believing no one could ever want me - even suicidal thoughts. It took years, but I had to learn to curb my imagination. Before I could begin to curb it, however, I had to recognize it was happening. I suffered a lot and experienced a lot of emotional pain before I began to realize my own mind was one of my main problems. To this day, there are still times when I must stop myself mid-thought. I had no such control over my thought life at this point in my life, though.

California

My aunt welcomed me into her home in Southern California and gave me a job in her dog grooming shop as a dog washer. I was a high-school graduate and she allowed me the freedom I desired. After I moved to California I dabbled in drugs, drinking and the care-free lifestyle of the mid-1970's. I had felt that Mom had been very over-protective as I was growing up, so the freedom I experienced there was exciting and liberating.

I washed dogs in my aunt's shop and met lots of fun people. I rode a bicycle everywhere and went to many parties with other young people. I always had a crush on one boy or another. I was still extremely shy though, so had difficulty developing and maintaining relationships. I could party all night with a guy without even speaking more than a few words to him. Fear was my prison. Fear and the inability to see well. I needed glasses, but vanity prevented me from wearing them. So, everywhere I went, my distance vision was blurred. This definitely had an impact on my actions and my ability to think clearly.

I was a typical example of a teenager in the seventies. I wore bellbottom pants and crop-top shirts that exposed my belly. My blond hair was fairly long and very straight. I had made myself a leather and macramé purse with long beaded strings that I carried around with me everywhere. I never watched the news or got involved with community events. In fact, I didn't even know about the Watergate scandal until I walked past a newspaper stand one day a few months after arriving in California and saw a headline announcing that President Nixon had been impeached!

I ran around with a guy for a while, whose name I cannot remember, who drove a cool "hippie" van. I thought perhaps I was in love until one of my girlfriends asked him in front of me if he was married and he said yes. I was shocked and hurt, but that is an example of how naïve I was.

It didn't take long before I began to feel like the California lifestyle wasn't for me. I allowed myself to be hurt by others and continued to suffer from shyness and the inability to stand up for myself. If someone hurt my feelings, I simply distanced myself from them and said nothing. I did have a couple wonderful friends who I cared for, though. I was happy to get reacquainted with them many years later through Facebook. Today, I

honestly can't even remember what all led me to believe that I didn't like California anymore.

In retrospect, I have since learned that when you are unhappy with yourself; you are destined to be unhappy no matter where you are. I had made a few friends, but I didn't always pick the best people to hang out with. I had my heart broken, I never expressed myself or stood up for myself in the ways I should have, and (shudder) I believed in fairy tales. I truly believed that when you got married you lived happily ever after. I decided I was going to return to Wyoming and settle down. I was ready to get married and find my happily ever after!

By now, I was nineteen years old, and it may have helped my decision knowing that back in the 1970's, the legal drinking age in Wyoming was 19. I went back to Wyoming and moved in with my parents. They had since moved out of Utah and back to Wyoming. Dad now worked at another dam. They lived in another extremely small town but was only a half hour drive to the largest town in Wyoming. Bear in mind, the largest town in the state still has a population of only about 60,000 people.

I loved that I could now legally drink with my dad! I adored being able to socialize, party and drink at the only bar in town with Dad. He was always so much fun! That period didn't last long, though because one night at the bar I met a tall, dark and handsome stranger!

I Believed in Fairy Tales

This striking man, whom I refer to in this book as "Ali," became my all-consuming interest. I have always been attracted to men with long hair. He had thick dark hair reaching down to his shoulders, called himself a Persian prince and after all, I did believe in fairy tales! He was smitten with this skinny blonde girl who was so quiet and shy. I soon learned much about the Persian country now known as Iran. At the time, all I saw was a gorgeous foreigner with a thick, sexy accent who WANTED me.

My parents were less than thrilled. Ali scared my mom. She always told me I was too trusting. I should have listened to her, but I was simply infatuated. I became instantly involved with him and we were married within three months.

I should also have listened to the reservations I began to have before marrying him, and I wish now that I hadn't been so insecure. I would have seen the signs that were right in front of me. I felt he was insanely jealous and possessive. When he was angry, he was violent and I was terrified of him. I learned to be very careful not to anger him.

I'll never forget the time we got a kitten. (My first cat, Cleo, still lived with mom and dad). The new kitten jumped out of the car one day and Ali had to run to catch it. I was horrified when he punched that little kitten in the face and bloodied her nose for running away from him! But, did I learn anything? No. There were signs, but I ignored them. I am frankly horrified today when I think of what all I tolerated.

One time, I was sitting in the car waiting for him on a day he was particularly angry about who knows what. I distinctly remember hearing an audible voice telling me to leave him. Whether it was God, or my future self, I don't know; but I literally told that voice, "but no one else wants me!"

Oh, the lies the mind can convince us of. Looking back, I was a pretty, blue-eyed 19-year-old blonde with a great body. But, did I realize that? No! My teeth were slightly crooked, I thought my breasts were too small, my belly was too big, my arms were too long, I was extremely shy and insecure, and he was a "tall, dark and handsome" man who wanted me. After all, I saw myself as a freak. My own big brother had told me often enough that I was ugly. He called me the "freak from battle creek." I can still remember studying my face in the mirror when I was younger and telling myself, "so this is what a freak looks like."

My insecurity led me to marry this 24-year-old Iranian who was in the United States on a student visa after a whirlwind courtship. Did I mention that he was previously divorced? I didn't realize until later that his first wife, also a blonde American girl, left him because of his violent tendencies. She was smarter than I was.

We did have some fun the first year despite his unreasonable behaviors. We worked together at local restaurants. He cooked and I waited tables. I was good at being careful to not do anything that might piss him off. I was very nurturing and cautious. Provided he got lots of positive attentiveness from me, and I didn't do anything to upset him, things went pretty well.

We worked at a very fancy bar/restaurant and coffee shop at the local airport for a while in 1976 shortly after we got married. One day, Anson

Papas with Ponytails

Williams, aka Potsy, from the popular seventies' sitcom *Happy Days*, was having lunch in the coffee shop with a friend. He had been my favorite character on the TV show, and my heart skipped a beat as I went to wait on him. I was still just a nineteen-year-old girl, and *Happy Days* was one of America's favorite shows at that time!

As I greeted them at their table, I noticed my jealous husband trying to hide the fact that he was spying on me through the window of the door to the kitchen. I didn't dare act friendly! Poor Anson. He was a handsome celebrity trying to flirt with this blonde teenage waitress in Wyoming and I didn't dare even smile at him! He seemed obviously disappointed that the charm he was trying to lay on me didn't seem to work. (*Oh, it worked all right. I still remember it more than 40 years later; but I didn't dare risk angering my jealous, scrutinizing husband*).

CHAPTER 4

Luke

From the time I was a young girl in high school, I always knew that one day I would have a precious little boy named Luke. I didn't know how I knew it, but I knew. I dreamt about him, prayed for him, and felt a strong bond with him before he was ever conceived.

Ali and I had been married several months when I discovered I was pregnant. I had always imagined the son I would have one day. I pictured him in my mind for years before he came into existence. His name was Luke, and I felt I knew him long before he was born. My dream came true in late summer of 1977. My precious son was born. I loved this little baby so much. He was small but it was still a difficult birth. They had done an episiotomy, but I still tore. I had to go back to the doctor later for even more stitches; it was not fun. I also had trouble breast feeding in the beginning. It hurt so much! My nipples were inverted; they bled and I shed a lot of tears, but I stuck with it! I nursed him for about nine months. Luke became my everything.

A couple months before Luke was born, we had financed a small plot of barren land outside of town and moved a trailer onto it. We put in our own septic system and I still remember trying to maneuver the wheelbarrow full of gravel with my big belly sticking out. I kept house while Ali worked. I recall that he did not want me to go out and be around other people at a

job where he couldn't watch me. He seemed to like having us live out in the country where I had no car or access to other people.

About seven months into my pregnancy I became terrified when it occurred to me that even if the baby died, I would still have to deliver him! Ali reluctantly agreed to participate in childbirth classes with me to help alleviate my fear. One evening, I had made sandwiches and packed a meal so that we could eat on the way into town to attend the classes. We didn't have a lot of time between his getting home from work and us leaving for the class.

I had tried to make a nice portable meal of ground meat sandwiches, chips, fruit and homemade cookies. I handed him his sandwich, unwrapping it for him so he could continue driving unencumbered. He took one bite and began screaming at me. He violently threw the sandwich, smearing it all over the inside of the car. He was enraged and I was frightened and confused. It turns out, I had failed to put mayonnaise on it. I accepted the blame, apologized profusely, cried, cleaned up his mess, and was eventually forgiven. Looking back, I now feel like I was the crazy one; for staying. This was just another example of how I witnessed his brutality and insanity.

Once Luke arrived, my husband was very resentful of the attention I gave the baby, but for once, I didn't care. He was jealous of the baby, he was jealous of my family, he was jealous of men who looked at me in the store. I didn't dare make eye contact with another man. I do know now that it was typical in Iran for women to always keep their eyes down, but I couldn't comprehend it back then. There were many times I got in trouble when we were in a store and he caught a man looking at me. I guess he always assumed I somehow purposely enticed them to look at me. I soon learned to make sure and not ever make eye contact with another man; at least not when he was around.

I can remember him getting angry once when I was taking him to a convenience store early in the morning to catch a ride to where he was working. I casually commented that there sure were a lot of people in the store for it being so early in the morning. He was angry for days but wouldn't tell me why. As I have alluded to before, when he was angry, he was surly, abusive and frightening. After several days of begging and crying on my part, trying to figure out what I had done, he finally told me. All those people in the store that morning had been men! I had actually been looking at men! I didn't even realize it at the time.

These are just a few examples of his petty jealousy and possessiveness. I couldn't even hug my own brothers! We had always been an affectionate family. Ralph and I were never as chummy after he married a woman who didn't like me, but Gene and I had always remained very close. He has since told me how hurt he was when, shortly after marrying Ali, I told him I could no longer embrace or show him physical affection when my husband was present.

Ali never allowed me to visit my family without him. Ali was actually jealous of my whole family. In fact, I can remember asking him if we could just drive past my parents' house so I could look at it. I missed them so much. It chokes me up a little even now thinking back to the fact that I longed so badly to see them that I got satisfaction out of at least looking at their house, knowing they were in it. Of course, I was afraid to tell my parents what living with this monster was like and he was always charming and pleasant around them.

My First Trips to Iran

Several months before Luke was born, I procured my first passport and we traveled to Ali's hometown in Iran so he could introduce me to his family. It was a long, exhausting flight; but flying in the late seventies was much more pleasant than it seems to be now.

My first Iranian food once we arrived, was a "hamburger" that made me ill. It was hand-formed, shaped more like a hot dog, and with my first mouthful, I bit into eggshell. Salt was in big chunks and it reminded me of grinding sand when it crunched between my teeth. I was suffering from the nausea of pregnancy and much of the food did not agree with me; but for the most part, I was fascinated with the new cultural experiences.

I adored Ali's mother. She was kind, generous and loving. His father was friendly, and I liked him, but I did notice he didn't do much besides sit and get waited on by his wife. They were both retired school teachers and owned a very nice three apartment home. They rented out the bottom floor apartment, lived on the second floor, and Ali's older brother, a dentist, lived in the smallest apartment on the third floor with his wife and infant son.

Cultural Differences

Mealtime was interesting. Everyone sat cross-legged on the floor to eat. They had a dining room table, but it was used more as a desk. They would put a tablecloth on the floor, set all the food in the middle of it, and everyone would sit in a circle around the food. A fancy dinner always started with fresh melon, berries and other fruit, as they said it "opens the appetite."

Meals generally consisted of a huge pan of rice with some sort of meat and vegetables buried beneath it. I do love rice, so I enjoyed it. (*I miss the days when my body allowed me to sit comfortably on the floor, though!*) Meals were usually served with a vinegar-based salad which included finely chopped tomatoes, onion, cucumber and spices, which I thought was a delicious accent to some of the other exotic flavors and tastes.

After dinner, the shot glasses came out…not for alcohol, though! A dark, rich tea was served in them. I'm sure they only considered them to be tea cups, but they looked like shot glasses to me. It was the best tea I ever tasted! Ali's dad taught me to put a sugar cube between my teeth and sip the tea through the cube - delicious and charming. Although we didn't speak the same language, his dad seemed to enjoy teaching me new things. He took me to buy bread early one morning. It was round and flat, much like the naan we see at Indian restaurants today and baked fresh daily in an outdoor brick oven. After pulling the hot bread from the oven it was wrapped in paper and we brought it home. This was a daily task for his father, so we had fresh bread every day.

I also remember waiting in front of the house with him for the salt man. A little old man came hobbling down the lane leading his donkey that was carrying saddlebags full of rock salt. We bought a large chunk of salt, took it to the rooftop, and crushed it up for use in daily food preparation. I found it fascinating.

The rooftop is also where the daily praying took place. At the same time every day, mantras of "Allah" were heard throughout the community.

Muslims wash their hands a certain way and face the correct direction to worship their God. Most men went to mosques for daily prayers, but when they couldn't go, they prayed on their rooftops.

In the area where we were located, homes and yards were surrounded by large brick walls. In walking around the neighborhood, I frequently smelled opium burning. This timeframe was after the shah of Iran had been usurped by the religious sector. Ali told me that opium had recently been made illegal, but the government rationed it out to elderly men who were addicted to it.

Toilets were another big culture shock for me. They were basically just a hole in the ground that you squatted over. Fortunately, his parents had 2 bathrooms in their apartment with an "American" toilet in one, and a fancy "Iranian" toilet in the other. In their Iranian bathroom the "hole in the ground" was porcelain covered with fancily decorated tiles. The "American" toilet was the raised type we are accustomed to seeing here in the United States that we can comfortably sit on. Most public bathrooms, or toilets, that I experienced there were disgusting. A filthy, urine and feces encrusted hole in the floor with a pitcher of water beside it to "wipe" with. I did my best to avoid using the public facilities while I was there. (*Granted, they may be better now than they were 40 years ago when I was there*).

I had a hard time understanding why women were expected to walk behind their men with their faces covered. I recall going on a walk with Ali one day shortly after we arrived for the first time, and he and his mother argued in Farsi before we left the house. When I asked him about it, he wouldn't tell me why they had argued. I found out after we had walked around in public and been stared at, that it was because I was going out with my head uncovered and had a shirt with short sleeves on! Looking back, I'm sure he was testing me to see if I looked back at any of the men watching me. I learned quickly and was careful to never make eye contact with a man there. The only dirty looks I remember witnessing were from the Iranian women. They must have hated me for exposing myself so blatantly!

In the United States we could walk holding hands, but while in Iran Ali refused to show any affection in public. At least not towards me; he could hug, kiss and walk arm in arm with his male buddies. I didn't like or understand it, but I knew I had to accept it and follow along behind him with my eyes down. This didn't help my insecurities.

I can't remember how long we were in Iran that first time, but it was at least a couple weeks. I do recall the segregation. Men and women were not allowed to sit together in mosques or even restaurants.

Drug Smuggler

Our second trip together to Iran occurred shortly after Luke was born. His family was thrilled to meet little Luke, and I was happy to see his parents again. I didn't go outside the house much on this trip since I had a baby to care for, so I was left alone in the house a lot while Ali was gone visiting his friends.

Ali dabbled in marijuana, but I had stopped smoking it when I first discovered I was pregnant. He knew he could make a lot of money in the states with opium and hashish, so he came up with a way to smuggle them out of the country. Of course, he used me as his drug mule! I think the timeframe was 1978. Baby wipes came in quite large, tubular containers which were much bigger back then than they are now.

As we were preparing to return to the states, Ali removed the wipes and filled the container halfway with a big block of opium. Since these containers were so sizeable, there was space for a considerable amount of the powerful substance. Opium has a very pungent smell, so he wrapped it up well in plastic before putting it in the container. Next, he melted wax over the top of it which helped suppress the strong odor. He then replaced the wipes, forcing them to fit back into the container, and put the plastic lid back on. He did the same thing with a large bottle of vitamins covering hashish that he also forced me to carry.

Due to the segregation of men and women, we had to go through customs separately as we were preparing to leave the country. Naturally, I had the baby, so Luke and I were sent through the women and children's line with the wipes and vitamins. Oh, the fear I felt when the customs agent picked up the opium filled vessel. My heart began to beat rapidly, and if he had been looking at me, I'm sure he would have noticed my eyes grow wide with fear. Curious, because he had apparently not seen such a

container before, he popped off the lid. I nearly had a heart attack right then and there.

When he realized they were baby wipes, he appeared embarrassed. He quickly pushed the lid back on and sent me on through the line without looking further at any of my items. Whew! What a relief that was! Looking back, I cannot imagine what would have happened to me had they found the contraband. Ali probably wouldn't have been in trouble; but I sure would have been. He sold the drugs for a pretty profit when we returned to the states. Of course, I never saw any of the money.

College

After our second return from Iran, Ali decided he needed to enroll in college again. Being married to me, he was now able to stay in the country without his student visa, but his parents had sent him to the United States for an education and he wanted to return to school. I'm sure his parents reminded him of that while we were in Iran.

We sold our trailer in the country and prepared to move to town. We were homeless for a few days while waiting for a student apartment to be available. Ali was too proud to ask my parents if we could stay with them so we "crashed" with an acquaintance of his. My cat Cleo had come to live with us by this time. It was winter in Wyoming and the people we stayed with wouldn't allow a cat in their home. I made a bed for Cleo in the car and hoped she would stay warm through the night. The next morning, I found her frozen solid. I was heartbroken and suffered intense guilt. My precious little comforter was gone, and it was all my fault.

Luke must have been a little over a year old by the time we moved into student housing at the college. I got a job at the phone company and worked while Ali went to school full time studying to become an engineer. This was before the phone company was automated. We sat at a big switchboard with cords that we would plug into it. Each cord represented a phone call. We fondly referred to our employer as "Ma Bell." I met a lot of awesome women there, but of course, the friendships were only while I was at work.

After the first year of school, Ali had flunked most of his classes and decided he didn't want to study any more. I think part of the problem was that he smoked a lot of pot. I didn't like it, so I abstained. At least when he was high, he was calmer, and nicer to be around, so I didn't say much. I was very careful about picking my battles. Fighting with him was never a good thing for me so I got good at biting my tongue and avoiding any sort of confrontation with him.

In order for us to continue living in student housing, he decided that I should go to college. I was still very shy and insecure, but also extremely unhappy in my marriage. The only joy in my life at that point was my son, so I was thrilled about the prospect of this new venture. Going to college was never discussed at the tiny high school I had attended, but it was always a dream of mine.

I am grateful that Ali rarely resorted to physical violence with me, but the emotional and mental abuse I experienced was horrific. I believe he would have been much more physical had I ever talked back or argued. Of course, walls and other items were physically abused. If he had broken a bone, maybe it would have knocked some sense into me and motivated me to leave sooner. Then again, maybe not. I tolerated holes being punched in the wall as well as lots of bruises and humiliation.

Who knows what all the reasons are for staying in an emotionally abusive relationship? I do know that I still tried to keep my mouth shut around my parents and acquaintances; not that he ever let me be alone with them. I was certain that the rage he directed at me was always my fault.

He was still doing what I considered to be crazy, insane things. Like when we had trouble getting little Luke to stay in his bed at night, Ali tied the door shut with a rope so Luke couldn't get out and I couldn't get in to him. He would get enraged if I fell asleep on the couch before he did while watching TV. I was expected to stay awake with him. I could never say "dinner is ready" at mealtime. He would decide when he wanted to eat, and the food had better be ready when he wanted to eat it. I got good at keeping food warm without burning it. These were pre-microwave days (at least for us). This meant learning to keep foods warm in the oven or on the stove without letting them burn or dry out.

Soon, his younger brother, who I will call Bud, had moved to our town to go to college. He and his American wife also lived in student housing and were our neighbors. They had a beautiful little girl who was just a little

younger than Luke. She told me once that Bud told her he would kill their baby before he would let her take his child away from him. Years later, she did leave him. Fortunately, she was able to take her daughter safely with her. I sometimes wonder what happened with her and her little girl.

I remember making a lovely Thanksgiving dinner one year for the four of us. After we finally sat down to eat, Bud announced with a whine, "I'm not really hungry." I was so hurt and disappointed after cooking all day. Ali was not upset with his brother, but he was angry with me for being hurt. Those are just small examples of what my life was like back then. Of course, Ali was always very pleasant and charming around other people. (*I am told that his brother today is a very kind and positive man*).

Surgery in The Third Trimester

I was taking birth control pills at this point in my life but missed taking one every now and then. I realized I was pregnant one day when the smell of frying hamburger made me nauseous. Following the typical lie that our minds tell us, I thought maybe another baby would help my miserable relationship. I was attending college by now, and Ali was working for the labor union. That meant calling in each day to see if there was a temporary job available. I hated him so much by this time. I didn't believe in divorce, but I wished he would die. How crazy is that; to wish someone would die because leaving is too scary?

In early December of 1979, when I was eight months pregnant, I woke up experiencing sharp pain in the lower right side of my abdomen. It didn't feel like contractions, as it was a constant pain that did not subside, and I was feeling quite ill and nauseated. By mid-day, I called my obstetrician. Dr. K was an elderly man with very old-fashioned ideas. When I described my symptoms, he suggested I make dinner for my husband and call him later that evening if the pain didn't subside. Sheesh. I struggled through the day and managed to make my husband dinner. By early evening, I was extremely sick. When I called Dr. K again, he begrudgingly told me to come to the hospital and he would check on me while he was doing his rounds.

I called my mom and she came to pick me up (since Ali had worked all day and didn't want to be bothered). Mom had worked all day too, but she didn't hesitate to rush me to the emergency room. Before Dr. K arrived, the on-call doctor ordered blood tests. Once Dr. K appeared, I felt he treated me as if I was faking or exaggerating my symptoms. I recall him arguing with the on-call Emergency Room doctor about my pain. The ER physician got angry with Dr. K for pushing on my stomach.

They had already taken the blood sample though, and as soon as the results came back, they rushed in to prepare me for emergency surgery. My white blood count was extremely high, and my appendix was about to burst. I felt that Dr. K was not happy with me about it.

I can still remember being in the operating room. I was extremely frightened. I hadn't had surgery since my tonsils were removed at age five. The medical professionals wanted to keep me awake for the benefit of the baby, so were preparing to do a spinal to numb my lower body while keeping me alert. As they were preparing me for surgery, a medical-masked man on my left was attentively trying to reassure me. He offered me his hand and I took it. My fear must have been apparent as he joked, saying, "don't squeeze too hard, I still have to operate!" I was surprised that the surgeon was already there with me. I guess this was the first time he would remove the appendix from a woman nearly nine months pregnant!

Somehow, with each pregnancy, I always knew what gender my babies were. I announced to the operating room staff that I knew I was having a girl. This was before ultrasounds were easily available and you could learn the gender before they were born. (At least I couldn't afford the procedure). At one point during the operation the surgeon announced, "it's a boy!" I was shocked! "Really?" I asked. "Well," he said with a chuckle, "it's a boy appendix." Humor is always good medicine!

The baby and I survived the surgery, but the next day I began to have contractions. My belly was full of stitches and looked like a football! I couldn't tell you today what it actually was, but they gave me a shot of what they called "male hormones" to stop my labor. It worked. After a few days, I was released from the hospital and returned home.

By this time, due to the pregnancy, surgery, and recovery, I had missed my final exams and Ali was still not working regularly. Nevertheless, we were calling the labor board for possible employment openings each day, even though there weren't always jobs available. All I really remember from

the time frame after my surgery was that he was angry with me for not being able to physically wait on him hand and foot.

I was huge with baby and my belly was full of stitches! If I laid on one side, the baby pushed on the stitches, and if I tried to lay on the other side, the baby pulled on the stitches. I was simply miserable. I felt I was living only for my children. Luke was everything to me. We had very little food and no money. I can remember times when we did have a few dollars, and Ali would go buy himself a new 8-track tape instead of buying milk. Of course, I didn't dare to complain due to my fear of the ramifications. I bit my lip a lot.

One day, after returning from a doctor appointment, I came home to a ringing telephone (*to those of you who are young, we had no cell phones, and the phone was attached to the wall with a long cord connecting the phone and the handset*). Ali was sound asleep, laying on the floor in the hallway near the phone. Apparently, he had gotten up when he heard it ringing, but fell back to sleep before answering it. I ran inside to answer the phone, and it was the labor union with a job! I had called them earlier in the morning to put his name on the daily roster.

The way it worked was that they would go down the list calling people who had previously phoned in to put their name on the log for that day. If someone was unavailable, or didn't answer, they would cross their name off and move down to call the next person. I begged them to wait five minutes before calling the next person on the list, saying that he would be back any second and would accept the job. They reluctantly agreed and I hung up the phone.

I begged him to wake up and call them back. I was desperate for him to take the job. We were out of money. We had very little food; not even milk for Luke. I didn't know about food stamps back then. However, I was also still in the mindset that I had to do what he said and to be careful about not making him angry. In my attempts to wake him, he screamed at me, "take that kid and the one in your belly and get out!"

I was shocked and thrilled at the same time. In that instant, I knew that was exactly what I was going to do! I loathed him by now but was still afraid of him. For once I would happily obey his command! I immediately turned and walked out the door with Luke. I ran to a neighbor's house

and called my mom. I'm sure it was a call she had been hoping for! She came right away to pick me up. (I was nice enough to leave him our car).

I was so very happy when I finally had the courage to leave him. Living with my parents again was a dream come true. My parents adored little 2-year-old Luke and were excited for the new baby. Luke was such a loving and good-natured little boy. I gained the courage to tell Ali I was not coming back and had my parents there to protect me. He tried to convince me to return but he couldn't deny that he had told me to leave. I was able to spend a glorious Christmas with my family, and my life was beginning to feel worth living again.

I went to Legal Aid and I filed for divorce. I should note that divorces in Wyoming are easily attained and the waiting period is only thirty days. Wanting to be a fair person, even though I was awarded full custody, I didn't want to deny Ali access or visitation to his son. I would let him spend time with Luke when I was there with them. I was naïve in that I actually thought he had accepted the fact that I was not going back to him. Thus, one chapter of my life ended, and a new nightmare was about to begin.

This was my life and events leading up to Luke's kidnapping and my trek to Iran during the Iranian Hostage Crisis to try and get him back. The following begins the new chapter of my life; when I left Iran without my precious son.

CHAPTER 5

Leaving My Heart Behind

People have often asked me over the years if I have ever seen the movie "Not Without My Daughter" which came out in the mid-nineties. They told me the book and movie were about an American woman who escaped a brutal Iranian husband with her little girl. I was often asked if I had seen the movie. My answer is no. The truth is, I got my daughter out, but I left Iran without my son.

I think I must have cried and slept the entire way on the first leg of the flight out of Iran that tragic day that I left without Luke, because I barely remember it. Since I was working with the Swiss Embassy, our first stopping point was Bern, Switzerland. Apparently, I had an advantage having worked with their embassy because we were late arriving in Bern and they held the flight to New York City until I got there. Bessie and I were escorted through the airport and taken to the plane. They seated us next to a large, middle-aged man in an expensive-looking suit.

He flew into a rage when they seated a young woman with a baby next to him. He demanded the stewardess find him another seat, preferably in

first class. I began to cry, which made him uncomfortable. He mumbled an apology and crassly said something about having work to do and didn't need the distraction. In tears, I explained I had just escaped Iran and had to leave my two-year-old son behind. He didn't know what to say, but he did show some sympathy for my situation. The stewardess returned to tell him they found another seat for him.

Apparently, this angry, self-absorbed businessman softened. Before leaving he turned to me and asked if I had any money. Of course, I had none. He proceeded to hand me a $100 bill. I was surprised and tried to turn it down, but he insisted I take it. I asked for his business card and said I wanted to pay him back, which he said was unnecessary. He gave me his card though, and I recall that his office was on Fifth Avenue in Manhattan, New York City. It may have been mere pocket change to him, but to me, it was a small fortune. This was a lot of money in 1980! In fact, according to CPI Inflation Calculator, $100 in 1980 was equivalent to $310.13 in 2019 (*Home Page*).

I would like to interject a note here about the nature of people. This seemingly cruel narcissist, once he learned about my situation, proved to have a heart after all. Everyone has good in them. Sometimes we must dig for it, but it is there. We need not be quick to judge. Someone related a story to me recently about a young man in a store with his two small children. The kids were unruly and loud. An offended bystander chided him to take control of his children and teach them some manners. He gazed at them with glassy eyes and apologized. "I'm sorry, he said quietly. "My wife just died and I'm kind of out of touch with reality right now." My point here is that we do not know what is on the other side of the moon. Don't be in a hurry to judge other people.

On the plane, Bessie and I were left with a whole row of seats to ourselves. I resolved to treat myself and bought a box of Swiss chocolates on the plane with part of that hundred-dollar bill. I decided not to open them until I got home so that I could give them as a gift to my family.

I gave the man's business card to Mom when I got back and don't know what became of it. I'm sorry I don't remember his name, but I hope we at least sent him a thank you note. Honestly, I was too distraught to remember now whether I actually thanked him or not. This is an example, too of the impact kind deeds can have on individuals. I still get choked

up when I think about his generosity and how much it meant to that frightened and distraught young mother.

I don't remember a lot from the next few weeks and months after returning from Iran. I know we went to a family reunion in Colorado shortly after my return, but I mostly remember it because of pictures. In the next few months, I was an emotional mess. Thank God for my parents. Bessie was loved, nurtured and well taken care of. I was trying to be a good mama but everything I did was overshadowed by the loss of Luke. I was relieved to be away from my tormentor, but I couldn't come to terms with the cost of that freedom being the loss of my son.

Ali was very angry when he realized I wasn't coming back. One time, I packaged up many of Luke's favorite toys, including a little rag doll that he had loved and carried around with him since infancy. I mentally saturated everything in the box with my love, believing that when he touched each item, he would feel my presence and know how much I loved him. When the package was returned to me rewrapped in new packaging, I was heartbroken. Ali had gone to the trouble of repacking the box to make sure I knew Luke didn't receive it. It felt as if he had been taken from me all over again. I shed so many tears during that period of my life. I can attest to the fact that it is possible to run out of tears.

In my deep sense of guilt, loss and devastation, I turned to God. I needed some sort of relief. Alcohol didn't seem to help, and since I was still breast-feeding Bessie, I needed to abstain from it, anyway. I had experienced a love for spirituality as a young girl so was easily able to seek God for comfort. I was desperate for a respite from my sadness and sense of guilt over leaving Luke.

The Church

There was a little church a couple houses down from where my parents lived, and I remember frequently listening to the music emanating from it. One day, I decided to go check it out. Turns out it was a church where they prayed in tongues and raised their arms in the air to worship. The minister of the church, who I will refer to as Pastor, was a wonderful, caring man. I experienced a lot of love and compassion in that church and Pastor was very instrumental in helping me turn to God and begin to experience some emotional healing.

I was still quite shy and insecure, and I clearly remember walking out of the church one day feeling sorry for myself because no one had come up to talk to me. I heard that familiar voice in my head again, asking me "how many people did YOU go talk to?" What a revelation! I realized I probably wasn't the only one leaving disappointed that day. After that, I always made sure I greeted someone no matter how difficult it was due to my shyness; especially if they looked sad or lonely.

I began to make new friends, and life went on. Pastor and his wife had three amazing kids, and their youngest child was the same age as Bessie. She and Bessie soon became fast friends and remain Facebook friends to this day.

His wife and I shared a birthday, and she was very nice, but I never got chummy with her. She told me once, shortly after we met, that God didn't believe in divorce and that I should pray for the restoration of my marriage. There was no way I could ever see that happening, so I refrained from confiding in her from that time on. We did maintain a friendly relationship, and I respected her, but I didn't allow myself to share with her or get close to her emotionally.

I remember telling someone whom I had just met at church one day that my son had been stolen and that I was in Iran during the infamous hostage crisis. She went on to become a good friend and later confessed to me that she thought I had been telling stories when we first met. In fact, she had gone to Pastor and said something about me being a compulsive liar. He told her my story was true. I learned to not tell people about my experiences after that, because they probably wouldn't believe me. To this day, people don't really learn much about my life and history from me until they have become a close friend.

I know I experienced some sanity and relief from the pain of losing Luke during my period at this church, but I personally don't put a lot of stock into the actual emotional healing that religion alone offers. I "accepted the Lord" as a young girl and loved God and spirituality for as long as I can remember. I always had problems with accepting the notion that there was only "one way" to salvation, though.

With the billions of people who haven't been "introduced" to Jesus,

Papas with Ponytails

and the thousands of forms of spiritual belief, Christianity to me seems like putting religion in a box. It is a wonderful form of belief, and I definitely believe we are spiritual beings; I just don't believe God sends everyone to hell that doesn't accept Jesus as their savior. I am a very spiritual person - I pray, I exude positive energy whenever I can - I just don't believe in "only one way."

During my time at the church I did believe that Jesus was the answer. Hey, all the images I ever saw of him were this handsome, long-haired man who loved me unconditionally! How could I not want to serve Him? After all, I had always been attracted to men with long hair! I grew up as part of a generation where many fathers, grandpas, and papas had ponytails! (*I've always loved papas with ponytails*).

As alluded to previously, this was a Pentecostal-type church, where they prayed in tongues, laid hands on the sick, raised their hands to worship, etc. There were requirements about the church I didn't like; such as not listening to anything but Christian music, but I could overlook that. I also chose to abstain from sex and alcohol for the church. These were not easy to give up considering I was a fan of both, but I tried.

All my life I was always infatuated with one man or another, but I was trying to stay moral. I had one friend outside the church. I can't even remember where I met her, but I think her husband worked with my mom. She had a little girl close to Bessie's age, and we began to spend a lot of time together. She wasn't involved with the church, and I was going through a period of confusion and depression dealing with my losses while trying to stay "righteous." I began hanging out with her more and more.

She re-introduced me to alcohol, and we drank together. Let's not forget that alcohol eased my pain and gave me confidence. I always "believed God" that Luke would be returned to me someday, but that didn't take away the pain and guilt over leaving him. I may have had remorse about drinking, but the pain of losing Luke was far greater than my guilt over drinking. We didn't drink often, but we did go out occasionally. While "partying" I could forget my pain.

One night, when we had gone out dancing, I met a guy who I was instantly attracted to. As we visited, I learned he was a musician and was also a religious man. I was thrilled! Here was someone who I thought must feel the same way I did; guilt over drinking but wanting to serve the Lord!

To make a long story short, we went home together that night. While we were in bed I announced "stop! I am going to get pregnant!" I don't know how I knew, but I knew. Well, we were both inebriated and we didn't stop. Afterwards, he proceeded to tell me that he was married. He already had two little girls and his wife was pregnant. He just knew God was going to give him a son this time. I promptly ended the encounter and grieved my actions. I returned to the church and gave up men and alcohol once again; convinced I learn my lessons the hard way.

Shortly afterwards, I was suffering from indigestion, which was unusual for me. I normally ate healthy and began to worry that I might have an ulcer or something. Well, one day I ate a taco and when that caused the pain to stop; I knew. I was pregnant. I then began a new trial in my life.

Little Lyle

I was ashamed and mortified to think that my very brief affair ended up with me pregnant (even though I suspected on the night I conceived; I didn't want to believe it). I now had to figure out what I was going to do next. Abortion was a possibility, but I didn't think I could go through with it, even though I am a firm believer in choice. I believe a woman should have the right to decide what happens with her own body.

Women can choose to give their baby up for adoption, but it is not an easy thing to give up a baby that you have carried under your heart for nine months. I admire any woman who can do it. Based on my own experience, pregnancy can be devastating to the human physique, and it lasts nearly a year! Every woman who carries a baby full-term is making a huge physical sacrifice. I always had difficult pregnancies.

You never know what the circumstances may be surrounding a pregnancy. Besides the corporal toll, having a baby is a lifetime commitment. Not all babies are born into a safe or happy environment. There were nearly 700 thousand children in foster care in the United States in 2017 *(Foster Care)*.

I considered abortion and adoption, but I had already lost one child; I didn't think I could endure giving up another one. My mom was mortified, naturally. Her good Christian daughter had gotten herself

pregnant! However, when I went to Pastor, he showed me much love and encouragement. (*He was a very kind and loving man who has since passed on. He is dearly missed by family and friends*).

I did go through a lot of emotional turmoil trying to decide what to do about this unexpected pregnancy, but eventually, I knew I was keeping my baby. I also knew, as I had with my other pregnancies, that I was having a boy.

It was another difficult pregnancy. I was sick a lot and each time I went to the doctor, he yelled at me that I was eating too much sugar, which showed up in my urine. I would cry, because I really was trying to avoid eating sugar. This was before medical professionals automatically did diabetes testing on pregnant moms. Diabetes runs in my family, so we should have suspected, but didn't. I had high blood pressure and various other complications, but my blood sugar was never tested. I ended up giving birth to a 10.5-pound baby boy, which, from what I have learned from being a diabetic myself, is a typical outcome of the high blood sugars of a diabetic mother.

In spring of 1982, after a routine weekly check-up, the doctor decided my blood pressure had stabilized to the point that I could be safely induced. I was admitted to the hospital around noon and he broke my water. The doctor assumed it would be a long labor, so he let me have a light lunch, which I soon regretted. Right outside my hospital window was a big revolving bucket advertising fried chicken, and I became very nauseous. (It was a long time before I could eat fried chicken again). The entire process went much quicker than expected and I delivered my baby within 3 hours of my water being broken!

Early on in my labor, I was asked if some nursing students could participate in the birthing process. I thought it should be okay, and appreciated the attention of the two students who waited on me patiently while I was in the labor room; rubbing my legs, feeding me ice chips, etc. I was shocked however, when I was wheeled into the tiny delivery room and there were at least two dozen or more students waiting to witness the birth!

I was freaked out, but not for long; pushing a baby out of my body took precedence over the discomfort of being surrounded by a horde of unknown observers. Due to his large size, the doctor and I had trouble birthing him. The baby's shoulders were stuck in the birth canal, but his head was already out, and he was turning blue. The doctor said he had to snap the baby's little shoulder in order to get him out. It took a few weeks before he could lift his arm due to nerve damage, but we prayed and worked with my new precious baby in helping him regain use of it.

I survived giving birth in a room full of strangers, but must mention that a couple years later, I was talking to someone about my experience, and lo and behold! They had heard all about it from one of the students who had been in the room that day! We knew it was me because the student told them the woman giving birth had previously had a child stolen and taken to Iran. At the time I wondered what happened to privacy.

I had not expected the birth of this baby boy to have as much impact on me as it did. Holding little Lyle in my arms for the first time, I felt healing powers entering my broken heart. I felt he truly was a gift from God. No one could replace Luke, but I was supernaturally comforted by little Lyle. He was such a good baby, too. I felt guilty for ever regretting his conception. I loved him with my whole heart, and little Bessie, now just over two, was thrilled with her new baby brother! She was such a sweet little "big sister" and our whole family was over the moon with joy. I let my dad (who was now deemed "Papa") pick out his name and he chose the name Lyle.

During my pregnancy, my dad told me "anyone can father a child, but I will be a father to this one." That meant so much to me, and he was a wonderful daddy to my children; as well as to me. Lyle still tells me Papa was the best father he ever had.

There is a lesson here for anyone who finds themselves unexpectedly pregnant. There may be a lot of fear and anguish in the beginning, but it will not last long. As I stated previously, I do believe in choice, and personally, I do not condemn anyone else for the decisions they make regarding their body, but if you and your family are able to go through with the pregnancy, you will love the child with all your heart. The fear and judgement will soon be forgotten. There are always exceptions with dysfunctional or abusive families, but I believe this is true with normal families. I have seen it many times.

I should add a note about the man who did father Lyle biologically, recalling that he had told me he knew God was "giving him a son this time." I saw him at a wedding when I was 9 months pregnant. We didn't

speak, but he left abruptly after seeing me, leaving his wife and three daughters at the event! (*I wonder; did I have the son he told me God had promised him?*)

Kelly

I met a tall, dark-haired, good-looking man I will refer to as Kelly at some point after Lyle was born. I honestly can't remember exactly where we met, but it was undoubtedly at a church function. We attended different churches that were similar in belief and were pretty much in the same circle of friends. He was a good Christian man, but he kind of got on my nerves. At one point, I thought of him as rather abrasive and annoying, as he definitely had a Type A personality; the opposite of my own. We began to hang out more and more, though, and eventually became friends. We would often spend time together along with other church friends, and my parents laughed that he "dropped in" for a visit every day at dinnertime.

Over the months, we began to spend more and more time with each other. One day, he came up behind me, put his arms around me and stated, "you are everything I want in a wife. Will you marry me?" As a young mother of two who was in love with the idea of love and marriage, I didn't hesitate to say yes. I was, after all, still a believer in fairy tales! Was I in love with him? Well, I was in love with the idea of love, so nothing else mattered. That was the first time we kissed, and we did not have sex until our wedding night.

I married Kelly in 1983. We bought a house together, and he proceeded to adopt Bessie and Lyle. I conceived a child within two months. Kelly was over the moon with delight. I recall him recounting a dream he had once where his future baby was lying in a glass box on the mantle over the fireplace. He claimed to love Lyle and Bessie as his own, but he never quite treated them the same way he did his biological child.

Things were great for a while, although I did have problems with his temper. He didn't get physical when he was angry the same way my first husband had, but he was a yeller. As I have stated previously, I always hated shouting. I guess he was as high strung as I was laid back. He was

accustomed to living alone and suddenly had a family of four – soon to be five!

I remember the first time he got himself an ice cream bar from the freezer and was upset that the kids then expected one. He didn't understand why he couldn't just have a treat when he wanted one without everyone else wanting one, too. Having an instant family was a big adjustment for him.

One thing I found annoying was the fact that so many people got our names mixed up. Since his name could be for a man or a woman, I was frequently being addressed by his name. I never heard anyone call him by my name, though!

Brief Return of Luke

When I was several months into my 4th pregnancy, I was blessed with the news that Ali was returning to the States with Luke and that he was going to come visit us. To say I was thrilled was an understatement! This was the miracle I had been praying for! Luke was six years old now and I was beside myself with joy at the thought of seeing him again.

Ali only allowed Luke to spend a few hours with me, even though here in the U.S. I had legal custody of him. Luke was equally happy to see his mama. He adored his little brother and sister and we spent much time hugging and playing. I don't even recall now how much, or how little, time I got to spend with him, but it wasn't long enough.

Kelly and his minister, another very kind and loving man, asked Ali to meet with us. We got together at the minister's house and they proceeded to tell Ali that God wanted Luke to remain with us in the U.S. and told him he should "do the right thing," etc. I don't really remember everything that was said, but I do remember that I could tell Ali was not in agreement. He said nothing, but I recognized his silent rage. Although he promised to bring Luke back the next morning, he disappeared with him during the night and I lost my child once again.

I could not forgive Kelly or his minister for (in my mind) chasing them away. Of course, I didn't tell them that. They put all the blame on Ali and his evil ways. I didn't have the confidence or verbal skills to argue with them. Who was I to argue with my husband and the minister? I

was heartbroken once again but consoled myself with the belief that God would bring him back to me some day and at least now he had a fresher memory of me in his mind and knowledge of how much I loved him.

Theo

I had been in pretty good shape physically when Kelly and I got married but was quite sick again during my fourth pregnancy. While I still didn't have a diabetes test, I gave birth to a 9.5-pound baby a week before my due date.

I had been in labor for 12 hours with my first child, my second for 6 and my third for 3. Naturally, I was expecting a quick delivery! I was wrong. I labored for 13 hours with Theo. Let me back up though.

Kelly's parents were very excited about the coming baby, but I felt his mom was controlling and possessive. A couple weeks before my due date, Kelly's parents decided to come from their home in California for the birth. His mother had what I considered to be a shrill, whiny voice that irritated me. Every day she nagged me; asking when I was going to have the baby. I hadn't even reached my due date yet. Looking back, I realize I didn't have a good perspective, but she made me feel like I couldn't do anything right and she felt Kelly was a saint. I got to the point where I couldn't take it anymore. I was desperate to have her stop constantly nagging me and was so ready for the baby to be born.

Extensive bumpy rides and long walks didn't seem to help, so my next step was to buy a bottle of castor oil. I had read somewhere that it could induce labor. It worked. I had horrible diarrhea after taking it and contractions soon began. It was a long, hard labor though, and I do NOT recommend it for other expectant mothers who are tired of being pregnant!

After an exhausting, painful 13 hours of hard labor I finally delivered Theo shortly before the 4th of July holiday, in 1984. I will never forget the words of Kelly's mother when she came into the hospital room and saw the new baby. In her somewhat piercing and annoying voice, she exclaimed, "Oh Kelly, you did such good work!" My reaction was, "Excuse me? He had the easy part! I'm the one who did the work here!"

Of course, the main reason I regret forcing the onset of my labor is

that Theo was obviously not ready to come. He was very jaundiced. This happens when a newborn's liver isn't quite mature enough to do its job properly. He had to be kept under the blue lights of phototherapy and was not released from the hospital as quickly as I was. Hospital staff allowed me to stay in the nursery with him though, especially since I was breastfeeding.

A few days after Theo delivered early, the day came that the minister's wife had scheduled a baby shower for me. I did not want to leave my new baby and wanted to stay with him at the hospital. She did not want to cancel the party she had worked hard to plan. She insisted that I attend. I was told by Kelly that I had no choice. I acquiesced, even though I cried on the inside throughout the entire baby shower. All I remember of it was missing and worrying about my baby. I had never been good at standing up for myself.

Eventually, I did get to bring my precious little Theo home, and all was well. Overall, I was happy with my family, despite the pain I always felt regarding Luke, and we were quite involved with the church. When we got married, I had been expected to switch to the church Kelly belonged to but it really didn't matter to me where we attended. I taught Sunday School, led bible studies, and assisted wherever I could. I had always enjoyed helping others. I was doing my best to be a good wife and mother, and with three small children, I was very busy! Life is full of changes, though and Kelly felt he was called by God to become a missionary.

CHAPTER 6

Costa Rica

Shortly after Theo's birth, Kelly told me he believed God wanted us to move to Costa Rica, Central America. At first, I was very opposed to the idea. I certainly did not want to move to another country where they didn't even speak English with three small children! However, being a good Christian wife, I prayed about it, and told Kelly if that is what he wanted, I would trust God and go along with his dream.

Foreign Language & Giant Bugs

By September of 1985, we had sold our house, packed up our children and moved to Costa Rica. The kids were now 1, 3 and 5. Once again, I broke my parents' hearts. I never fully realized back then just how selfish I was. It's only since I have had my own children and grandchildren move and live far away that I can see how much I hurt them. At the time, it was a frightening, yet exciting, new adventure.

We decided that we would attend a language school in San Jose, the capitol city of Costa Rica. Our first home was a tiny, two-bedroom house with no hot water, which was common there. They had special cakes of dish soap that made suds in cold water, and showers that had a small electric heater at the top of the shower head, which heated the water as it

came out. They were called "widow makers." You learned to be careful not to touch the device during your shower!

There were lots of cockroaches and other disgusting bugs that were deplorable to this Wyoming girl. Wyoming has bugs, but due to the long, cold winters they don't keep growing larger year-round. Bugs in the tropics are huge and I have many stories I could tell. We also didn't have much money, so I had to learn to use food sparingly. I still remember when ants got into the container of our precious sugar. We couldn't afford to throw it out and buy more. No, I banged the canister on the counter a few times and moved it to a different location on the outside patio. It didn't take long for the ants to depart and I used the sugar.

Another time, Kelly opened the living room curtain and a huge 6-inch cockroach with wings was resting between the folds. He ran to get the bug spray. I told him "No! Bug spray won't be strong enough! Get something to hit it with!" He didn't listen to me and he proceeded to douse it with an insane amount of powerful bug poison. I swear, that roach slowly turned its head around as he proceeded to soak it with the smelly liquid, and locked eyes with him. It gradually began to flap its wings and suddenly made a beeline right for his face! He screamed and jumped about a foot in the air! I thought it was hilarious! He ended up hitting it with something to get rid of it. He wasn't happy with me for laughing at him, but I couldn't help myself. It was funny, even though I was creeped out.

I had pretty good night vision when I was younger and was accustomed to going to the bathroom in the dark at night without turning on a light. After finding a roach on the toilet seat one time, I learned to make sure I turned the lights on whenever I got up to pee. Bessie still remembers waking up during the night to see the floor moving with bugs. We didn't waste much time in looking for a different house. That one had more than an average number of roaches and other disgusting bugs.

On a positive note, we met a wonderful Costa Rican family that lived around the corner. The wife spoke some English, and they were very helpful in teaching us many of the traditions and culture. I still smile when I think back to a time when we were eating dinner with them at their home. Kelly scooped up a ladle full of chicken soup and had a look of shock when he saw a chicken foot glowering up at him from his bowl!

They laughed and told him he didn't have to eat it; that it was mainly in the soup to add flavor.

Our first Halloween in Costa Rica was while we lived in that house. I didn't know what to expect. Kids didn't really dress up like they would in the states, but they did go door to door pleading for treats. Since they didn't know English, they squealed "Halloween" instead of "trick or treat" which I found to be endearing.

Costa Rican Food

Coffee was the number one export in Costa Rica, with bananas coming in a close second. Coffee plantations were amazing, and they had banana trees growing intermittently among the coffee plants to help create shade. I was not a coffee drinker when we first arrived in Costa Rica but felt compelled to drink it while I was there, since it was such a valuable commodity. I soon fell in love with it. Back in the days when I could drink milk freely without physical side effects, my favorite was *café con leche.* After a nice meal at a restaurant, servers would bring not one, but two equal sized pots of hot liquid. One was their rich, aromatic coffee, and the other was fresh, creamy, steamed whole milk. I would pour the same amount of each into my coffee cup. It was so delicious!

I remember wanting to go for Mexican food once when we were visiting the U.S. Someone chuckled and said, "I guess you got used to that kind of food, huh?" After a moment of confusion on my part I realized they didn't comprehend the fact that Mexican food is only found in Mexico! The most common meal in Costa Rica was black beans and rice; with lots of garlic, but nothing spicy.

Tamales were also very popular. Tamales were not wrapped with corn husks as we are accustomed to in Mexico and the United States, though. In Costa Rica, they are wrapped in banana leaves. We heard a story once about when President John F. Kennedy came to visit Costa Rica in the 1960's. Upon being served a tamale, he proceeded to try and slice through the banana leaf and eat it. The people telling us the story were delighted by it. Christmas tamales were a special holiday treat when they added raisins to the filling to make them more festive.

Avocados, bananas and other fruits there were wonderful. I remember well when I returned to the states for a visit once and picked up a banana. I peeled it back, took one bite and instantly stopped. "Oh my gosh!" I said to myself as I peered closely at it, "what is wrong with this banana?" I realized it tasted flavorless because it had been picked green and not allowed to ripen naturally as they are in Costa Rica. The sweetness was gone. I still don't care much for bananas in North America.

A good example of how fruits and vegetables begin to lose their flavor after being picked is something my dad always used to tell us about corn. "The best way to eat corn on the cob," he would say (and do!) is to start the water to boil on the stove, then run out to the garden and pick it. The longer you wait to eat it the less natural sugar it has." I find these words of wisdom to be true with all fruits and vegetables!

Beggars were a bit of a culture shock for me. I realize now that beggars are found all over the world, but having grown up in Wyoming, they were new to me. They were abundant in the larger city, and one time I watched a woman on a street corner gather up about a dozen children who appeared to be bringing her all the things they had collected for the day. They had huge bags of items. Whenever beggars came to our door, I would find some sort of job for them to do in return for food and/or money.

Hopefully, anyone who has ever gone to Costa Rica has eaten "Pop's" ice cream. Pop's (pronounced like the Catholic pope) is a popular ice cream shop there that has a multitude of flavors of ice cream, gelatos and treats made with the delicious fresh fruits and other delicacies of Costa Rica. They had more flavors to choose from than anywhere I have ever been.

We experienced fruits in Costa Rica that I had never seen before. One house we rented for a short time had a tree in the yard which produced one of the tastiest fruits I've ever eaten. They were called "*manzanas de agua*" (water apples). I've never had them anywhere else and still remember their delectable juicy taste. They were simply delicious, but I have never seen them since. I assume they just don't keep well, are only ripe once a year, and are only found in certain tropical climates. I would love to be able to find them again someday. If I had the financial means, I would search the world just to taste their mouthwatering essence one more time.

Another fruit that was new to me was the cashew fruit. I have always loved cashew nuts, but never knew that the nut is actually the poisonous

stem of a fruit. The nut needs to be treated and roasted before you can safely eat it. The fruit could be found at roadside stands during its period of ripeness. The locals said that it rots very quickly. It was mainly used to make a juicy drink. I could go on and on about all the amazing fruits there. Returning to Costa Rica someday is definitely on my bucket list!

Speaking Spanish

After the first few weeks, we realized we could only afford for one of us to attend language school. I went for a couple months and got some basics, but I literally knew NO Spanish when we first moved to Costa Rica. I probably knew *"adios"* (goodbye) and *"gracias"* (thank you). I knew *"si"* meant yes but didn't realize that an accent over the "i" meant the word was "yes" and no accent meant "if". I loved the language though and threw myself into learning it.

One of the beneficial things about Costa Rica was the fact that live-in maids were very inexpensive. I recall one American friend I had made who, when we were just beginning to learn Spanish, told me that her floors were getting pretty dirty (no carpeting in Costa Rica). She kept telling her maid *"por favor, limpia las flores"* but she kept coming home to find her floors were still dirty. It wasn't long before she realized *"las flores"* meant the flowers! Once she realized her mistake, she also noticed the plastic flowers on her table were really clean!

After being there a year or so, our income had increased. We weren't rich by any means, but eventually we were able to afford the few dollars a week for in-house help. In fact, a live-in maid cost only $50-80 per month, which included housework and childcare.

I tried to use Spanish every chance I got. They say immersion is the best way to learn the language, and it is definitely true. I practiced it all the time and forced myself to try and think in Spanish. Before long, I was even dreaming in Spanish. I ended up learning the language faster than Kelly, who was attending language school. Granted, he probably learned more correct grammar than I did, but if we were with someone who spoke both languages, Kelly spoke English. I always used my Spanish when conversing with someone who spoke both languages.

I did go meet with a Spanish tutor a few times. Once, when I was getting ready to leave the house, Lyle looked up at me with his big blue eyes and asked, "Mommy? Are you going to see your gasser?" He thought I was going to see a "tooter" rather than a "tutor!" I had to laugh! (*I wonder what he thought we did there…*).

We met some wonderful people while we were in Costa Rica. I learned to love almost everything about it despite the giant bugs! I loved the climate, the culture and the people. We were involved with a large church group in San Jose that had a lot of other American missionaries working with them. For a while, I even taught part-time in a local English-speaking Christian school. I remember well the day I was working there and someone came into the school to tell everyone that NASA's space shuttle Challenger had just exploded. It was a tragic day, indeed.

One time a local family begged us to come visit them and when we did, they proceeded to fill a pitcher with water from the river behind the house. They poured us each a glass, squeezed half an orange into it, threw in a handful of coarse salt, and served it to us. We learned quickly to bring a bottle of soda with us when we visited some of the poorer areas of town. They may have been poor, but it was good manners to serve us something. It would have been rude to turn them down if we hadn't already had a drink with us. Getting parasites was common there. Fortunately, we didn't need doctor's prescriptions to get medicines.

We often hosted visitors from the U.S. and found opportunities for them to help others and show them around the country. We also helped set up temporary clinics and we had healthcare professionals come and serve in some of the poorer areas. It was very rewarding work and I loved being a translator!

Climate

Some of the most beautiful sights I have ever seen are in Costa Rica. In fact, the word "lush" to describe vegetation had no real meaning to me until I witnessed the flourishing Costa Rican scenery. I've never been to Hawaii, but I was told that (at least in the late 1980's, when I was there) Costa Rica is as beautiful as Hawaii, but without all the people.

Papas with Ponytails

Temperatures were in the high 70's to low 80's almost all the time. I didn't notice the humidity while in Costa Rica, but I sure felt the dryness each time I returned to Wyoming. The rainy season lasted from about July through November; being the worst in October and clearing up in December. We learned to carry an umbrella with us every day during this season, which was not a normal activity for this Wyomingite. The only time we got that much moisture in Wyoming, it was in the form of snow. On an especially rainy day in Costa Rica, the watery pellets came down so hard, you would be soaked from the feet up to your chest just from the rain that splashed up under the umbrella! I loved it.

The weather during the first three months of the year was the most beautiful; thus, the tourist season. We made several trips to the beach when we could. Our favorite vacation spot was Jaco Beach. We learned to ask for a hotel room higher than the first floor, as fewer bugs showed up in our temporary living quarters. I always said if I were to live on the beach there, I would get a pet iguana to help control the bug population. Iguanas there were huge, easily 4-5 feet long and they ran around everywhere; much like the squirrels do back home. There were also monkeys in the trees, and huge, colorful tropical birds flying all around. It was absolutely a tropical paradise.

The beach-front hotel that we preferred had a beautiful outdoor pool with a little island in the center of it which our kids enjoyed. After spending all day in the ocean and the pool, followed by a hot bowl of fresh seafood chowder before bath and bed, the kids slept great. We all had a blast and a tropical beach is still my favorite place on earth! One of the best parts for us was that these mini vacations were very inexpensive.

One time when we were at Jaco Beach with a visiting youth group from the states, there was a televised international surfing competition going on. It was a lot of fun, but I recall Kelly being quite stressed trying to keep the teenage girls we were responsible for away from the surfers. You can just imagine how thrilled those small-town Wyoming high school girls were with all those handsome surfers!

Life in Costa Rica

I previously mentioned a house we once rented in the country for a short period of time. It was a great old house and we had a lot of visitors from the states that we took there. One time we took the previously mentioned youth group to spend time with us at the house. I had so much fun with those teenagers. (*Little did I know then, that I would end up working with teens years later*). Bessie remembers the time she was sleeping in the attic with the teens and woke up to their screams. A bat had flown into the open window and they were all freaking out. The bat was eventually chased out and no one was hurt, but it was an exciting story for those kids to take home.

Another time at that house, when Lyle & Theo were five and three-years old, we had gone for a walk and the boys stopped to check out an ant hill. Now, this wasn't a typical ant hill like you would expect to see in the States. This ant pile was almost as tall as the boys, and consisted of dried grass, sticks, and other residue collected by the hardworking ants. They were also quite large ants; at least an inch or more in length. I was standing nearby watching them. The boys were on either side of the anthill when Lyle became curious about what would happen if he kicked the pile.

Lyle tells me now that he told his little brother they should see what happened if they both kicked it at the same time. Lyle moved a little faster than Theo though, and when he gave that pile a good kick it blew debris and shocked ants all over his little brother! Theo shrieked as he was being bitten by the distressed creatures and I rushed over trying to brush them all off him. He began to swell up.

Here we were, in a foreign country, far from medical help, and our young son's life was in danger! Fortunately, a woman from Florida was there visiting us with her husband, who was a police officer. She had some potent antihistamine medicine on her. We gave Theo what we considered an appropriate dose and his swelling subsided. What a scare that was. Lyle is still teased about the time he almost killed his little brother!

Palmita

The first live-in maid we had, who I remember fondly, was a Nicaraguan woman named Fern. She was a lovely, dark complexioned woman with an adorable little girl named "Carla" who also stayed with us. We were continually working on finding areas of service when she introduced us to her American boyfriend who was the director of a Nicaraguan refugee camp a couple hours from San Jose.

Eventually, he granted me permission to come into the camp as a preschool teacher there. We moved from the capitol city to a tiny barrio called Palmita and began working at the camp. One interesting fact I learned about Costa Rica while we were there, is that the country is well educated. Every barrio, no matter how small, always had a school. Usually, each community also had a central park. The town park would be surrounded on each side by the school, a market (grocery store), a Catholic church, and (of course) a bar! Something for everyone! This was the case in Palmita.

Our first home in Palmita was what I called a glorified grass hut. It was constructed out of bamboo, and the roof was thatched with palm fronds. It was beautiful! There was a two-room oversized loft, where Fern and the kids slept, a large living room, a kitchen area, and a small enclosed bedroom where Kelly and I slept. Our bedroom and the bathroom had four walls with a window, and the loft was walled in on three sides with a half wall facing out over the living area. The kids slept with netting over their bed to keep the insects away.

The rest of the house was built with walls of bamboo with open spaces for windows. It was quite impressive. Except for the bugs. One time a huge beetle flew into the kitchen and landed on the counter. Kelly picked up a big butcher knife and whacked that beetle as hard as he could with the sharp, wide end of the blade. That bug was so big the knife stuck in the middle of his back! I still recall being somewhat horrified.

Bessie was our only school aged child and we decided to send her to the local elementary school. She did a good job of communicating in Spanish and made some sweet little friends. However, when we found out the teachers were not requiring any work from Bessie due to the language barrier, I proceeded to home-school her.

One little friend of Bessie's gave her a baby chick. It was the ugliest little chicken I have ever seen; a breed with no feathers on its neck. Bessie loved that bird though and named it Sarah. Neighbors soon also gave Lyle a chick that was fully feathered. I have memories of the two chickens perching between the bamboo poles in the open aired kitchen, watching us while we cooked, and snacking on the tiny creatures that flew in.

Speaking of birds, I will never forget when Kelly brought home two live turkeys a couple months before Thanksgiving. We didn't have a pen or space for them, and I was not happy about having them. Especially since he got the big birds specifically for Thanksgiving dinner! The children were excited though, and not really realizing what we meant when told they were for Thanksgiving, promptly named them "Thanks" and "Giving." I had to tie ropes onto their legs and tether them in the yard to keep them from running away. Kelly couldn't seem to understand why I wasn't as excited about the turkeys as he was.

We had moved out of the glorified grass hut by the time Thanksgiving finally rolled around, but we still had those birds. I told Kelly if he gave me a turkey that was plucked and cleaned the way I would get one from the store in the states, I would cook it. As Thanksgiving neared, the day came that Kelly decided to prepare one of the turkeys for dinner. The kids were excited about whatever was about to happen, and they all gathered around their dad. I can still see it clearly in my mind and will attempt to describe the event as I remember it.

First, he hammered the tips of 2 nails about a half inch from each other into a small rectangular piece of wood. The idea was that he would put the turkey's neck between the nails and twist them together to hold the bird's neck down while he chopped off its head. He proceeded to trap the head between the nails, then reached around to pick up the knife. Bear in mind, he was using one arm to hold this big bird down. Every time he reached for the knife with his other arm, the bird popped its head back out. I remember finding it hilarious and we were all laughing (except Kelly).

However, the amusement turned to horror when he finally succeeded in whacking that turkey's head off. The kids were mortified! I still remember the looks of shock on their little faces. With everything we had done and discussed, they still hadn't fully realized that daddy was going to kill their

pet turkey! There were tears and cries of disbelief as the turkey ran around wildly with its head chopped off.

Kelly plucked and cleaned it though, and I ended up cooking the bird even though I refused to eat it. We had friends over for Thanksgiving dinner who all said it was delicious, but I also made a chicken (that I had purchased cleaned and ready to cook) for me and the kids. I guess it's apparent that I didn't grow up on a farm. I have known many people who grew up in the country, that have told me all about having to eat their pets. We ended up giving away the second turkey while it was still alive.

San Isidro del General

The new house we had moved into was a few miles down the road from Palmita and was in a town called San Isidro del General. Although it was nowhere near the size of the capitol city of San Jose, this town was much more populated than Palmita, and the house was larger than our glorified grass hut. It even had a small grass hut-like gazebo in back. This house was fully enclosed and had a full kitchen, 3 bedrooms and a maid's quarters, so Fern and her daughter had their own room.

"*Estadounidenses*" (people from the United States) were well liked in Costa Rica, but Nicaraguans were not. The fact that we were working with Nicaraguans and had one living in our house did not make us very popular in the neighborhood. I didn't care what the neighbors thought though, and we made friends through our church work. We began attending an outdoor church and became very involved. We had several young adults who enjoyed working with us and we spent a lot of time together. We moved a couple more times while living in San Isidro; each time to a little bit nicer home.

One day, shortly after we moved to San Isidro, Theo got sick. He had a high fever and went into convulsions. Kelly picked him up and rushed him on foot to the nearby local hospital. As the medical staff worked to get his fever down, they decided to run tests. I actually fainted when they began to insert a needle into his spine! I woke up in another room, and at first all I could think of was how much I wanted my mom!

The conditions in this country hospital left much to be desired. All the

children in the pediatric ward were housed in the same room in dormitory style beds. At mealtime they hauled all the sick children to the same cafeteria and seated them together at a long table. Breakfast was coffee and bread! Most of the kids were in for snake bites but many were very sick. I remember one child vomiting in the middle of the floor, and it seemed like hours before anyone cleaned it up.

After a couple days with very little improvement, we decided we should take Theo to the city of San Jose, which was about a three-hour drive. Medical care in the capitol seemed to be much better than in the small towns. When we attempted to take our son out of the hospital, their staff refused to let us take him. They claimed that while he was in their hospital, he was their property. That is one time I was glad to have a husband with a strong, overbearing personality! Kelly went ballistic on them. How dare they try to tell him he couldn't take his son! After he threatened to get the U.S. embassy involved, they reluctantly consented and allowed us to leave with Theo.

When we got to San Jose, the doctor diagnosed Theo with an infection and sent him home with a few doses of penicillin. We were staying with friends there and after a couple doses, he was as good as new. He had been given penicillin at the country hospital, but we realized they must have been diluting the doses to save money. Bessie says she still remembers us chasing little Theo around the house when it was time for him to get another shot.

About a month after Theo was in the hospital, we were in the states for a visit and discovered Theo had contracted Hepatitis A, which we assume he got from the awful conditions in that hospital. Fortunately, our family never had any more hospital experiences during our nearly four years in Costa Rica.

We had a few pets while we were there. I mentioned the turkeys and the chickens, but at one point we got a little baby duck for each of the kids. They were the cutest little things! Bessie named hers "Grammy Duck" after my mom. Lyle dubbed his "Papa Duck" for my dad, and with a little help from his dad, Theo christened his "Habakuk Duck" after a book in the Old Testament. The ducklings enjoyed cuddling and being held and they loved playing in the rain! It was adorable watching them run around in circles lifting their little duck bills up to the sky to catch raindrops. At

some point after they were grown, we gave them to another family that had a farm, where they had more space to wander.

Not long after moving to Costa Rica we bought a German Shepherd puppy we called "Bibi." Bibi was a cool dog, and we have many fond memories with her, but I especially remember how she would always let us know when an earthquake was coming. She would bark excitedly and run around in circles. It amazes me how animals can sense things like that!

We also acquired an adorable kitten that Bessie named Miracle. So named because she said it was a miracle her dad let her get a cat! She also remembers her little brother throwing the cat off the balcony at our house to see if it would land on its feet. (Fortunately, it did)!

Refugee Camp

There is much information out there about Nicaragua and the Sandinista Revolution and Contra Wars. I could write an entire book on the events of that period. However, while we were in Costa Rica working with Nicaraguan refugees, I was relatively ignorant when it came to world affairs and all the politics and conflicts of the time. I do encourage readers to research the history for themselves, if interested. In this book, rather than citing long lists of controversial articles, I am just going to relate what I learned at the time from what the refugees told me about their own struggles and suffering. I heard first-hand accounts of how these people were tortured and abused. They lost their homes, their farms, family members, peace of mind, dignity and so much more.

When we were first allowed entrance into the refugee camp, it was so that I could teach preschool. I don't think the director really cared what we did, though. There weren't many people wanting to do anything to help the residents there. Kelly came to the camp with me and soon began providing church services. We got to know many of the refugees during our time with them. Once we began working in the camp, we learned much about the hardships and difficulties these people had endured.

According to the stories they told us, many of them had owned land in Nicaragua. They were farmers without a lot of money, but who were rich in their own ways. They had been busy with farming the land, raising

their families and animals, and minding their own business when the Sandinistan armies invaded.

They told us that the soldiers destroyed their crops, stole their animals, raped their women, killed those who did not comply, and took over their lands. They forced young men to join their armies. We were shown the scars from bullet wounds on the refugees' children.

These are the things that cause people to pick up what little they have left and leave their own lands looking for safety for their families. Costa Rica accepted many refugees, but that doesn't mean the general population liked them or treated them particularly well. I'm grateful Costa Rica did open their borders and give them refuge, though.

While we heard of refugee camps nearer to the coast where the conditions were worse than the site we worked at, it was still appalling there. Families were given a very small allotment of meat once per week. When a baby was born, they were given one piece of cloth to use as a diaper. Fortunately, there was a stream nearby, so they had "running" water. This was their only source of water for drinking, washing, etc. For the most part, they were warm and welcoming to us, and we tried to help them as best we could. (*I have since met many ungrateful Americans in my life that I would like to send to a refugee camp for a couple weeks. I think the experience would be a good attitude adjustment for them*).

Our work in Costa Rica was supported by friends and churches back in Wyoming, and we returned at least once a year to share about the work we were doing and to raise more support. The kids have fond memories of staying with my parents "Grammy and Papa" during those periods.

One of our first big fundraising projects for the refugee camp was to raise the resources to purchase sewing machines and material so the refugees could make clothing and diapers for themselves. Our next project was to construct a building for pre-school and church. We were able to raise the funds for supplies and the skilled refugees erected the building. They used it for school, church services, meetings, and more. We would travel to the refugee camp during the day and return to San Isidro in the evening.

Kelly preached and performed ceremonies and I taught the children basic hygiene, reading and writing, stories, songs, etc. We had young adults from the local outdoor church we attended in San Isidro helping

us. Eventually, we aided the refugees in learning to do all these things for themselves.

Not all our experiences there were good ones. One family we were devoted to, had a daughter about Bessie's age. The two little girls frequently played together. One night, when we weren't at the camp, their little girl became very ill and she was rushed into town and taken to the hospital by a staff person. The family wasn't allowed to go with her or even visit her at the hospital and they contacted us the next morning for assistance. When we went to the hospital to check on her, we learned she had died during the night. We were heartbroken, and sadly, we had to tell her parents. Naturally, they were devastated.

We never did find out why she died. We bought them a little white coffin, in which she was carried by a long line of mourners to where she was buried. The coffin, I remember, was too small for her, but it was the only one available. I will never forget the unnatural way her little legs had to be twisted in order to fit her into the casket. Kelly performed the funeral services and we grieved with the family.

There were happy times at the camp, too. They always seemed pleased to see us when we came to visit. I loved hearing the refugees' fond memories, love stories, and tales from their farming days. Overall, they seemed to make the most of their circumstances and were accepting, kind and loving to us. They had lost their homes and so much more, but at least now they were safe. They had found refuge. Occasionally, some individuals or families found work on a nearby farm and were able to leave the refugee camp.

As I stated before, they only got a small allotment of meat once a week. One time, Kelly hit a huge iguana with the car on his way to the camp, so he threw it into the back of the vehicle and took it with him. The residents accepted it with gratitude and feasted on it! We witnessed an iguana being cooked one time over a wood-burning stove. They had sliced it's belly open from neck to tail and stuck a stick inside to open it up. You could hear the crackling and sizzling as the juices ran down into the smoking fire. I must admit, I was relieved when they apologized that it wasn't ready to eat yet.

Another time, when we showed up at the camp to visit a family, they had just made tamales. They wanted to share them with us. Now, we had plenty of food ourselves, and certainly did not want to take theirs, but

they insisted. Culturally, it was an insult to turn down food or drink that was offered, so we reluctantly consented. We said we would just share one, though. They proceeded to hand us a metal bowl with a plump tamale in it and two small misshapen spoons. It was tasty, but I felt guilty eating their sparse food.

At one point, Kelly uncovered a lone piece of precious meat. One look told us both that their meat that week had been pork. Staring up at us from the bowl was the outer nostril of a pig snout; complete with short strands of whiskers! I'm sure you can imagine our reaction! With wide eyes, Kelly pushed it towards me and said, "you can have this bite." I looked at him with disapproval, pushed it back with my spoon and said, "oh no, YOU have it!" We didn't want to offend our hosts, so when they weren't looking, he quickly scooped up the snout bit with his fingers and stuffed it into his pocket! I can only hope they didn't see what we had done. That was, no doubt, a choice morsel for them and they had bigheartedly offered it to us!

Transportation

The refugee camp was built deep in the rain forest and when we first started traveling there, we would take a long bus ride to the turn-off, then walk five miles in on the narrow dirt road. It was a long, hot walk, but I was in great shape! Shortly after beginning our work at the refugee camp, we were able to raise enough money to buy a used Toyota Land Cruiser. It was crude and rugged, but we were thrilled to have our own transportation. We could bring refugees to town or to the doctor now and go back and forth much more easily.

Having transportation saved us a lot of time that had previously been spent on the bus or walking. Mind you, the rural busses were not pleasant experiences. The city bus system in San Jose wasn't as bad as the rural, country busses, but at least there was a means to get around. I rode a lot of busses during my time in Costa Rica!

I will never forget the time I fell asleep on the hot, dusty bus full of people. After walking several miles to the bus stop in the hot sun after spending the day at the refugee camp, I was very weary. As is typical when someone falls asleep, my mouth dropped open. I woke up to the sound of

Papas with Ponytails

people laughing and discovered a rolled-up piece of paper had been wedged between my open lips. Kelly thought it was hilarious as he entertained everyone on the bus by sticking the paper in my mouth. I was embarrassed and humiliated and don't think I ever got over what was, in my opinion, a total lack of respect for his wife. To this day, I am very self-conscious about falling asleep in public for fear of my mouth dropping open. I won't even allow myself to fall asleep on a long airplane flight.

Getting the Toyota Land Cruiser saved us a lot of time and was a real blessing. The car was very basic. It had two seats in the front with an open area between them and a bar along the front for holding on to for support. The back had a bench seat with no seat belts. It was a rather rough ride; but it beat walking and taking the bus everywhere!

One time we were heading to visit a refugee family that had procured work outside the camp. They were living rather far from civilization. We were bounding along on a dirt road and Theo, who was probably three, was standing between his dad and I as we drove along. Theo was holding on to the front bar for dear life as the car bounced up and down. I will never forget his earnest little face as he turned to me with a look of uncertainty and asked, "Mommy? Are we having fun yet?"

Another time, I was with a couple of young Costa Rican guys that we had been working with as we took a group of refugees into town. I allowed one of the Costa Ricans to drive our car since he wanted the practice. Suddenly, someone yelled, *"Hay un animale"* (there's an animal!) He stopped the vehicle and we jumped out to see what sort of strange animal we were beholding at the edge of the rain forest. We were about thirty feet from it when we realized it was a giant tarantula! I was amazed! I was also sorry I didn't have a camera with me!

If you saw the giant spiders in the Harry Potter movies, you can imagine what this hairy guy looked like. It was at least three feet high and more than four feet in diameter! I wanted to catch it! Fortunately, the two Costa Rican blokes were holding me back, telling me they are called *"mata caballos"* (horse killers). One bite and a horse would drop dead. I guess I was trying to be the *"gringa valiente"* (brave woman). The truth is, if that humongous spider had taken one foot in my direction, my whole façade would have been over. We watched one another warily for a few minutes before the arachnid turned and disappeared back into the jungle. The

tropical rain forests of Costa Rica are said to have insects and amphibians that are not found anywhere else in the world.

While living in San Isidro, our maid Fern moved on and we soon hired a woman named Teresita. She was an angel. We all adored her, and she was wonderful with the kids. Bessie told me once that when she would wake up frightened in the night, she would go to Teresita's room for comfort.

We were fortunate to have Teresita, but she was grateful to be with us, as well. I remember the first time we had her sit with us at the table for a meal. She was accustomed to being treated like hired help, but we treated her like family. She enjoyed cleaning, cooking, spending time with our kids, and she loved ironing. I had to tell her not to iron the bedsheets, but I did compromise with her by letting her iron the pillowcases!

Teresita was probably in her mid-thirties and never married. She stayed with us during the week and left on Saturday to spend Sundays at her parents' home. We invited her to return to the States with us when we left Costa Rica, but her father told her no. I still think of her fondly and would love to find her again someday.

More Machine Guns!

In early 1988, tensions were rising between the United States and Panama. Nonetheless, I had the opportunity to attend a Christian conference in Panama City. In conflict with Noriega, the Panamanian ruler at that time, the U.S. government had frozen economic and military aid to Panama and I once again experienced the fear of men with machine guns (*Jenkins*). The banks in Panama City all had armed guards standing outside them. As I walked around the city with a group of people, and we neared the bank, the guards pointed their guns at us as a warning to stay away.

This was also during the Nicaraguan Sandinista/Contra wars. On my return from Panama, the Costa Rican airport was fogged over, and our airplane was unable to land. We ended up flying further north to Managua, Nicaragua. As we got off the plane, there were Sandanistan soldiers with machine guns throughout the airport. One armed soldier threatened me with his machine gun when I tried to take a picture of him

with my camera. To make matters worse, it was determined that we would have to spend the night there.

I was assigned to a room with a mentally unstable woman I didn't know who was really freaking out. She spoke only Spanish and my own Spanish was certainly not perfect. The only way I was able to calm her down was to read the bible to her in Spanish. I read and read and read until she finally fell asleep in the wee hours of the morning; "*la madrugada*", as they called it in Costa Rica. I was exhausted.

I showed my own small act of rebellion the next day though, when I took pictures from the airplane window of the armed soldiers. I have no idea where the pictures are today, but they were taken with a cheap camera anyway and weren't impressive. Fortunately, we finally made it safely back to San Jose that next day. (So, I have had machine guns pointed at me in three different countries)!

End of A Chapter

We had a lot of great experiences in Costa Rica, but I was very unhappy with my relationship. Looking back, I suppose I sought approval that I wasn't getting from my husband. Kelly and I had terrible communication (in my opinion) and I didn't know how to make it better. I was often attracted to other men, although I never acted on my impulses. I remember one handsome Costa Rican man who gave me lots of attention. He even told me once that he was in love with me. I knew nothing could come of it, but it stroked my ego. I have never been unfaithful to a man, but it is easy to be tempted when you are unsatisfied.

We did do much good work and helped many people during our time in Costa Rica, but I had begun to feel like a hypocrite. In 1989, after working nearly four years in the country, I decided Kelly and I needed to focus on our relationship. I was experiencing much inner turmoil because I was so unhappy with my marriage. Shouldn't being honest and sincere in every aspect of your life be a major part of doing God's work? Being angry and dissatisfied with my relationship while accepting funds from supporters and representing Christianity just didn't feel right to me.

I loved Costa Rica and the people, and didn't want to just walk away,

but I was very discontent. To make a long story short, I told Kelly we needed to return to the states to work on our marriage. I felt we were frauds since we were supposed to be doing God's work, yet I was so unhappy in the relationship. I felt like I was living a lie and I couldn't continue to do so.

Later, I learned a lot about what was wrong with ME and what MY part was in my unhappiness…but at the time, I thought Kelly was mainly to blame.

CHAPTER 7

Alcohol And Freedom From Religion

How do those two things go together?

"In my mind, if Jesus rejected me for choosing to leave my miserable relationship, then alcohol welcomed me with open arms!" Alcohol became a salve that soothed my rejection of religion.

Return to the States

What were some of the things that caused me to be so unhappy in my marriage? In my opinion, Kelly yelled too much at the kids, and I felt he was unreasonable in his discipline. It felt like such hypocrisy to me when he would yell at the kids all morning in preparation for an outing, and then change his character completely as we walked into the church or public place and he proceeded to greet people with a warm smile. Things like that frustrated me, but I had taught myself to not say anything.

He was much more competitive than I was. He didn't like that my Spanish was better than his, and after someone once told us that I gave a better presentation than he did, he no longer wanted me to present

with him on our speaking tours in the U.S. Of course, these were my perceptions. He may see or remember things differently. As I said, we had very poor intimacy and communication skills. I had learned in my first marriage to keep my mouth shut when I was angry or hurt.

When I had told Kelly that I wanted to return to the states to work on our marriage, he didn't seem to think we had a problem. His answer to everything was to "pray about it." Eventually though, he reluctantly agreed, and we moved back to the states.

By the time we returned, it was the middle of a cold Wyoming winter. Despite the dramatic change in our lives, we ended up not doing any counseling other than with the minister of the church we had been attending. I don't really remember a lot from that initial period, but one incident in particular convinced me I was finished with the marriage. It was a freezing cold, snowy winter and Kelly decided he was flying to Phoenix to "do a gem show" with an American friend we had met in Costa Rica. It was so cold in fact, that the motor on our car froze up before he left.

Here I was; in a cold house (after living in the tropics) with three small children, no money…and the car was frozen! To make things worse, he was in warm, sunny Phoenix, Arizona (which is where our money had gone) having a great time! I decided that was the last straw. I was "done." I had a friend whose father worked with Legal Aid at the time. She was unhappy with her marriage, too. She hauled me into his office, and I still remember her saying in her little girl voice, "Daddy, we need divorces." Uncontested divorce in Wyoming is an easy process, and it didn't cost me a dime.

When I told Kelly that I was finished with the marriage, he was understandably resistant. I didn't believe that he wanted the marriage to work because of his undying love for me, but because he didn't like the status of being divorced. He wanted us to meet with his minister. The same man who (in my opinion) had helped chase Ali away with Luke several years before.

I can still clearly remember that very emotional conversation. Well, conversation denotes the idea that we were all talking. In my perception, I just sat and cried as they lectured and preached at me. Basically, I was told that Jesus would not be happy with my decision. My ultimate response to this, with my heavy heart, was "you're probably right, so…screw Jesus

then." I was finished. In my interpretation, if my freedom meant I had to turn away from God, then so be it. I walked out of there hurt, angry and determined. In my mind, if Jesus rejected me for choosing to leave my miserable relationship, then alcohol welcomed me with open arms!

I only drank on the weekends that I didn't have the kids, but I partied a lot when they weren't around. My memories of that time are hazy, but I did try to be a good mom whenever I had the kids with me. My mom was pretty upset with me initially for my decision to leave Kelly, but she and Dad lived in Arizona by this time, so we only spoke on the phone.

Somehow, Kelly convinced me to let Theo stay with him during the week while I had the two older kids. Looking back, allowing this eased my guilt over hurting him, I guess. After all, Theo was his blood child. It broke my heart, though.

Again, alcohol helped to ease the pain and guilt. The kids told me that their dad was telling them to pray that we would get back together. I was sick and tired of being wounded by people who said "God told them to" do whatever they did to hurt me.

One example was a friend who was spending the night with me before I had rejected God. She decided to leave in the middle of the night to go home without waking me up. That didn't bother me, but what did bother me was that when I woke up, my car was gone! I was late for work the next day because "God told her to" take my car in the night. Of course, I "accepted" her explanation without saying how I really felt. I had many examples of being hurt by people who claimed they were doing what God told them to do. How could I argue with them when God had told them to do it? These things all contributed to my resentment of God and religion.

It wasn't long after Kelly and I divorced that I was doing secretarial work and bought my own house. I always had a job, but I did drink on the weekends that I didn't have the kids. I had dated a couple men, but I certainly wasn't looking for anything serious. For the most part, I thought I was happy. Whenever I felt guilt over rejecting God, or in thinking about the pain of losing Luke, I would just have a drink and it would ease my pain.

At one point, in a period of regret, I decided I would turn things around. I would repent my sins, accept Jesus back into my life, and work on restoring my relationship with my ex-husband. Before I confessed my change of heart to Kelly however, I learned that he had met a woman at his church that he was serious about. So, I said nothing and continued to reject God, and drink the pain away. Kelly remarried within the year.

Time heals, and I slowly began to get myself back emotionally, although I was still finished with the whole "religion" thing. I still experienced tremendous emotional pain whenever I thought about Luke, but I had a good job, was a responsible homeowner, and became what I considered to be a "normal" drinker. As I stated before, I only drank on the weekends I didn't have the kids. I tried to be a good, loving mom and I truly loved my children. If you ask any of them today, they would all agree on that.

Custody Battle

Not long after Kelly remarried, he and his new wife, who had custody of her two children, decided they were moving to another state. They determined that they wanted to take all five children with them. The idea of him taking my kids away was preposterous to me. I was a good mom! I did regret ever letting Kelly adopt Bessie and Lyle, though. I felt that was a mistake on my part; in my eyes, they were MINE, not his. Not long following my divorce, my parents moved back to Wyoming when Dad retired from the U.S. Bureau of Reclamation. They sold their costly Arizona home and bought a nice less expensive house within a block of mine. They could live much more comfortably on their retirement in Wyoming than they could in Arizona. They also wanted to be near their grandchildren, and it was wonderful having them so close.

In response to Kelly and his new wife planning their move, the father of Kelly's wife's children decided he did not want his kids to leave the state, so he sued for custody of his children. So basically, Kelly was suing me for custody of our kids while his wife was being sued for custody of her kids. Kelly and his wife had the same lawyer for both custody battles. Mom and Dad helped me hire a lawyer and we were certain we didn't have much to worry about. Of course, it was a stressful time, but we were confident we would win. After all, I was a good mom and by this time, had a good steady job, and owned my own home.

I won't go into details about the courtroom experiences, but they

were not pleasant, to say the least. Kelly and his lawyer fought dirty. I was naïve. He got a former friend of mine, who attended his church, to testify in written documents that she had come to my house during the night and found the children alone, which was completely untrue. I had never ever left my children alone. I couldn't believe that this "Christian" friend would lie so blatantly. At the time this supposedly occurred, she and I were living together in her townhouse before I bought my own home. She was the same friend who had taken me to see her daddy about divorces that worked with Legal Aid. On the rare occasion I did go out while my kids were home, it was after they were in bed, and she had agreed to babysit. Of course, it was written in court documents so was accepted by the court as true.

Kelly apparently drove past where I lived, writing down the license plate numbers of cars parked in front of my house "at all hours" to try and prove I had questionable behavior by listing people with criminal records who were parked there. I lived next to an apartment building! I always had random cars parked in front of my house! He even brought in the unstable ex-wife of someone I had casually dated to testify that I had interfered in their marriage, which had ended before I even met the guy.

Of course, these lies were documented in the paperwork the judge saw but weren't brought up in court. I was shocked at the maliciousness of the lies and allegations against me. Especially since most of my accusers were supposedly "good Christians."

My parents and I suspected we were in trouble after the first morning of the court proceedings when we went to lunch with my lawyer and he asked my mom how she thought he was doing. It turns out, he was insecure and inexperienced. Sadly, a few years later he committed suicide. He didn't really do anything to fight for me in the courtroom, but I still felt very badly when I heard that news, as he seemed to be a very sweet man.

When the judge gave his verdict, giving Kelly custody of my sons, he stated that his "reasoning" for awarding Kelly guardianship was that they would get better discipline if they lived with their father. I was devastated when custody of Lyle and Theo was given to Kelly and his wife. I could not believe it. The judge let me keep Bessie, but I found out afterwards that when the three kids met with the judge during the trial, she was the only one old enough to stand up for herself. She told the judge she would

rather go into foster care than live with Kelly. You'd think that would have had an impact on a fair judge's decision regarding the boys, who were too young to have to make a choice between their parents.

Soon after my loss, Kelly and his wife then actually lost their custody battle with her ex. They had the same lawyer for both cases…and the same judge! I found out later, that judge almost always awarded custody to the fathers. In fact, I was told, his own wife had abandoned him and their children years before. He had raised his kids as a single father, so typically awarded to all fathers.

There is so much to be said about all this, but I remain speechless about the irony and fate involved here….and how it dramatically affected the lives of me and my children. Bessie told me recently that Kelly had told the kids it was God's will that they be with him and that I would be better off without them! I think that is a horrible thing to tell a child. I was definitely NOT better off without them.

To make a long story short, Kelly and his wife moved away with my boys. They had to leave her two kids behind. I was absolutely devastated. If they thought my drinking was an issue before, losing custody of my kids sent me over the edge. I don't remember much from that period because I was in so much pain. In my mind, I had two more sons "stolen" from me. Bessie had also gone with them for summer visitation, so suddenly, all my kids were gone. I proceeded to fall apart. Of course, I never got counseling. Alcohol was my only comfort.

Another Chapter in My Life

A man I will refer to as Peter had moved to town to work in the warehouse of the business where I was the secretary. I had been seeing a couple guys at different times during that summer but didn't plan on getting serious with anyone. Pete was just concluding a relationship and ended up moving in with me. Shortly after we got together, I learned I was pregnant.

He was thrilled at the time. I met his family, and we prepared for a life together. I can't say that I was madly in love with him, but he wanted me, and I was pregnant, so I made a personal commitment to him. I

was still insecure enough that someone "wanting me" was grounds for a relationship. He was grumpy most of the time, but I had experience with, and was good at, pleasing disagreeable men. He didn't care for my family and especially didn't like my kids, but he went to work every day and helped pay the bills. He drank a lot, but we got along well for the most part. The center of our relationship was my pregnancy. I soon learned I was diabetic.

By the 1990's, doctors routinely did a diabetes test on expectant mothers. They check your blood and make you drink this nasty sweet liquid and check your blood again in an hour or so. They checked my blood, had me drink the vile stuff, and sent me out to the lobby to wait an hour. Meanwhile, they got the results and found my blood sugar was nearly 500. A normal blood sugar is 80-120. They didn't make me wait an hour. They immediately sent me to the hospital where I ended up spending a week learning how to treat myself with insulin. At the time, they assumed it was gestational diabetes, but I know better now. Years later I was diagnosed with adult onset Type 1 diabetes, which my father had.

Cross Between Insanity & Salvation

At one point before my pregnancy, I had often said I didn't want another baby unless I had a guarantee it was a girl. Not because I don't like boys, but because I already had three boys and only one girl. Of course, once I was expecting, it didn't matter what the gender was. As with all my previous pregnancies, I sensed it was a boy before I was very far along. I allowed Pete to pick out the name, since this was his only child and I had four already. He considered naming him after his favorite NASCAR driver, since he was an avid racing fan but he was also a baseball fan. Being from Colorado, he decided to name the new baby after the Colorado Rockies baseball team that had just been established.

I was 36 years old by the time Rocky came along. I have always said Rocky was a cross between my insanity and my salvation. I was crazy to be having another child. There are nine years between my two youngest children. However, I completely stopped drinking. I began to take better care of myself and was excited about this new life inside me.

I was closely monitored during my pregnancy due to my health. I don't recall the name of the doctor who treated me, but he was wonderful, and I really liked him. He was a gentle, caring young man finishing up his residency, and treated me with dignity and respect; which was rare in my personal experiences with medical professionals.

It was determined that Rocky was breech near the end of my pregnancy so the doctor decided that, coupled with my diabetes, it would be in my best interest to plan a cesarean section. My due date was nearing, and the doctor was preparing to go to a conference for a week, so we decided to set the date for the Friday before he left town to make sure he would be present. A C-section is great when it comes to bypassing the pain of labor, but the recovery took much longer than a natural birth. Part of it may have been my age and disease, but my recovery from the surgery was rough compared to the previous four natural births.

In May of 1993 my precious baby boy was born. Pete proposed to me while we were still in the hospital. It seemed like the right thing to do under the circumstances, and we soon had a lovely small outdoor wedding at a friends' cabin in the mountains.

I was breast-feeding again, and Pete seemed jealous of the time I devoted to my new baby. As previously stated, he really didn't like my family or my other kids. At least it seemed that way to me. It wasn't long before things began to turn sour between us, and most of it was fighting about my kids. He still drank a lot and would get surly and angry when he drank. Bessie remembers him embarrassing her as he hung out of the window, drunk, hollering at her and her friends.

One thing I did like about Pete was his pet snake. He owned a 12-foot boa constrictor that was an awesome serpent. She was very gentle, and we held her a lot. She only ate once a month or so and we bought rats for her to consume. Sometimes it was difficult to find live rats when we needed them, so one time we bought two at the same time. Naturally, by the time the snake was ready for her second meal, we had named the rat "George" and he had become a pet. I remember calling Pete at work one day in tears telling him "George got eaten today!" After that, we bought frozen rats to feed her.

The process of feeding a large snake is cool, though. We would put the rat in the snake's glass cage and wait for her to be ready to devour it.

When ready, she would wrap herself around it, and squeeze the life out. Once it had suffocated, she would unlock her jaws and slowly inch her mouth around the animal until it was completely consumed. It took a couple weeks for the large lump inside her to be digested. Pete filmed the process one time and Bessie took the snake and the video to school for a science report. Bessie said it was the only time she got an A+ in that class!

Before Rocky turned 2, we attended a company Christmas party where the owners put all their employees up in hotel rooms for the night to counteract drinking and driving. My parents were our overnight babysitters, and as I wasn't accustomed to drinking any more, I didn't do well handling my drinks. I left the party early and went to the hotel room and to bed. Pete didn't return to the room until the wee hours and it wasn't until much later that I learned he was having an affair with a married co-worker.

I only had Lyle and Theo part-time since they now lived out of town, but Bessie was a young teen and going through typical teenage girl hormones and rebellion. It got to the point where I began to once again dislike my husband. Of course, I was not a good fighter. Piss me off, and instead of screaming and yelling and getting it out of my system, I would walk away and not talk. This is a great recipe for resentment, although I didn't realize it at the time.

We argued more and more often, and my resentment towards him grew. It got to the point where one night, during a disagreement, he told me to choose between him and Bessie. I laughed; at least on the inside. For me, there was no choice. I would choose my kids every time. I told him as much and he left. I found out later his lover left her husband, and as far as I know, she and Pete are still together. As much as he had grumbled and complained about going to functions with my family, he admitted to me weeks later, that he actually missed doing things with them.

While I was relieved to no longer be in an unhappy relationship, I felt horrible that I was going through a third divorce. I was ashamed of it and came down hard on myself. I certainly didn't want to be with Pete anymore but wondered where I had gone wrong with my life, to have failed yet another relationship. It wasn't until years later that I realized I was marrying out of insecurity and not for love. Once again, alcohol welcomed me with open arms.

Alexandra Flowers

My First Grandchild

By the time my divorce from Peter was final, I had a good secretarial position in an art museum and really liked my job. Bessie was 16 and had moved in with her fiancé when they came to my office one day to let me know they were expecting a baby. They were very excited about it. Her fiancé was a wild one; he shared his name with a wild west outlaw and was a few years older than Bessie. Bessie was a beautiful, charming 16-year-old girl and had many male admirers. Her fiancé was in and out of trouble, and soon wound up incarcerated in a half-way house/prison facility where you could leave each day to go to work but had to return at night.

They had planned to get married before they knew about the baby and I helped Bessie plan a lovely little wedding in the park. She didn't get to see much of him unless she visited him at work since he was incarcerated in the evenings. We suspected they were in trouble at their wedding reception. My dad pointed out how much the groom played and flirted with the other girls there instead of focusing on his bride.

Bessie called me in tears on her wedding night when she had discovered evidence that he had been cheating on her. He claimed the "sexually transmitted creepy crawlers" were from a dirty toilet seat…but we knew better. Her marriage was not consummated and ended before it had really begun. Bessie was able to easily obtain a divorce and little Beau was born a few months later, a few days before Christmas of 1996. Bessie was living with my parents when Beau was born and she was an amazing little mama. Of course, she had "practiced" a lot since she was thirteen when Rocky was born.

I remember coming to visit Bessie in the hospital the day Beau was born. I was trying to defy the fact that I was forty. Showing up in my leather jacket and skinny jeans with my long blonde hair, I considered myself to be a pretty hot grandma. Of course, I also brought homemade cookies. I looked into the big brown eyes of my new little grandson and made a vow to him on the day he was born that I would always be there for him and look out for him. A few months later, I finally got clean and sober.

Bessie left a few months after having Beau to participate in a Job Corps program in Kansas designed for single parents. She and Beau did well there and Bessie received her GED and culinary training.

Drugs

After my third divorce, before Beau came along, I had started out drinking casually, just as I had in the past. But it soon became a huge part of my life. There were always people at my house, and many of them were Bessie's friends. Fortunately, we didn't have police beating on our doors, but I did learn later that my house was considered a "flop house" by local authorities. It wasn't long before I was introduced to meth. Methamphetamines mess with the pleasure centers of the brain. They made me feel wonderful, and having lost all interest in food, I quickly got quite thin. In fact, my entire ordeal with meth lasted only a few months, but it was enough for me to destroy myself further than I ever had before.

I hooked up with an attractive younger man that I had met a few years before, and he didn't waste any time moving in with me. I know now that he saw me as a new, safe place to hide. He sold drugs from my house; and I actually felt flattered when he took me around and introduced me to his dealers and customers. I don't remember who any of them are now, because it was so long ago, but I do remember the spiral downward.

There were always people staying at my house. At first, I resented the fact that I was the only person living there who had to get up every day to go to work. My solution? I quit my job. I was told that it takes at least a year before you lose your house once you stop paying the mortgage, so I stopped worrying about paying it. I'm not sure how I got by.

I still managed to be a mom to Rocky and could pull myself together for the short periods of time that I had the other boys, but they lived out of town now, so it wasn't very often. Bessie, who was pregnant, wanted nothing to do with everything that was happening in my house. She house-hopped with friends for a while but eventually moved in with my parents. They lived close by and she still visited me regularly and spent a lot of time with Rocky.

I don't really remember when I learned that methamphetamine worked much better when it was injected directly into the bloodstream, rather than snorting or smoking it, but WOW – I thought it was great! I used to joke that being diabetic, I was taught how to stick myself with needles, but honestly, you don't inject insulin into the vein. I also stopped worrying about my diabetes. I never checked my blood sugar levels. I rarely ate, so

figured I didn't need insulin. I just didn't care and did nothing to treat myself. Insanity is definitely a consequence of addiction.

I wasn't a fan of marijuana at that time and drank much less alcohol when I had access to meth. I got an abrasion on my eye once from being awake for several days. I was keeping my eye covered with a bandana because even the slightest light caused intense pain. After suffering for a week or so, someone handed me a joint and told me to take a hit. I was shocked when, after only one toke, the pain in my eye was instantly gone. After that, I began smoking it regularly; especially when I needed to come down off the meth.

Coming down off meth is extremely painful and uncomfortable to say the least. Pot made a huge difference in soothing that process. As is typical of the insanity of using, I can remember bragging to myself that I never used all three of my vices at once; marijuana, meth and alcohol. A powerful sense of false pride is another of the many ugly byproducts of addiction.

Meanwhile, my drug dealer boyfriend beat me up and "broke up" with me, but just moved to a different room in the house. He treated me horribly; and worst of all - I let him. He pretty much chased all my friends out of the house, so only his buddies were there now. Our twisted relationship became more and more vile and I continued to spiral downwards.

Methamphetamine is the most addictive and destructive drug there is. It leads to loss of appetite, insomnia, significant weight loss, and much more. The caustic chemicals used in producing this illicit drug causes users to experience paranoia, aggressive behavior, confusion and a rapid deterioration of a person's behavior and appearance (*Methamphetamine*).

I got to the point where I felt like I was losing my mind. I would actually go hide in my closet, rather than deal with anything – or everything – that was going on around me. The boyfriend, being particularly nasty to me one time as I was falling apart, said with disgust, "I thought you had a back-bone!"

There are times in our lives when words go into the ear, through the mind, and straight into the heart. It was like God shot me with a dart. That was exactly what I needed to hear. "I thought so, too" I told myself meekly. That was the first step towards realizing and actually accepting that I needed help. I finally broke down and went to my parents, who encouraged me to go to the doctor.

I went to someone I had known a few years previously when we served together on the American Diabetes Association Board of Directors and told him I needed to get off meth. At that time, there was a treatment ward in the local hospital, so he admitted me. Today, I don't even know how the hospital bill got paid, although I do have a faint memory of completing paperwork requesting financial aid with someone from the billing department.

This was undeniably a turning point for me, although I lied about my addictions. I never mentioned alcohol, was put on Prozac, spent a week or so in the hospital, and went home feeling a flicker of hope. I never refilled the Prozac prescription, but was still smoking marijuana (which I felt was the only way I could relax), and I continued to drink moderately. I was proud of myself for giving up meth but was still in a pretty wretched emotional state.

It wasn't long before nonpayment of my mortgage finally caught up to me, and I was forced to leave my 4-bedroom, two-bathroom home. I simply abandoned my house. Although I didn't appreciate it at the time, a neighbor stepped in and bought my house for what I owed on it. Thankfully, I was never sued and didn't have that on my record. Rocky and I moved into a tiny apartment. While living in this apartment, I finally made a real step toward recovery.

CHAPTER 8

Recovery

At a turning point in my life, I walked into my first meeting of Alcoholics Anonymous in April of 1997. After one of my first meetings, I went home, opened a bottle of beer, drank a couple sips and threw it out. I told myself, "I can stop after one drink; maybe I'm not a real alcoholic." Then, I proceeded to roll a joint and light it. I soon realized I could do without one vice only as long as I still had another.

I needed to try and stay away from everyone I knew who was using drugs, which wasn't that difficult since they all thought I was a snitch now. They were still consuming illegal substances, suffering from paranoia, and suspicious of everyone. If I wasn't using with them, they presumed I was "telling" on them. I actually gave away the last of my meth and marijuana. I was much better off without them, anyway. I still wasn't emotionally capable of holding down a full-time job, so had the time to attend meetings every day. Fortunately, there were numerous meetings all over town.

People in meetings told me it is good to do 90 meetings in 90 days. I did at least twice that many. After one of my first few meetings, I went home, opened a bottle of beer, drank a couple sips and threw it out. I told myself, "I can stop after one drink; maybe I'm not a real alcoholic." Then, I proceeded to roll a joint with pot and light it. I soon realized I could do without one vice only as long as I still had another.

Spice

I did a lot of things wrong in the beginning. We were told to stay out of relationships for the first year of recovery, so of course, I picked a cute male "sponsor" and slept with him right away. I kept going to meetings, though. The longer I stayed sober the better I got at making healthier decisions.

I was told that I needed a real sponsor and that in order to pick one, I should listen to what others said in meetings, and find someone I felt I had something in common with. Soon, I met a beautiful free-spirited woman at a meeting who went by the name "Spice" that I felt I could relate to. One of the things that attracted me to her was the fact that she was usually barefoot. I had fought with my mom my whole life about not wanting to wear shoes. I asked Spice to sponsor me.

Up until that point, I had given up the meth and the alcohol but was still smoking pot. Spice told me that I didn't actually have a sobriety date until I gave up EVERYTHING; meth, alcohol, AND marijuana. I thank God for her now. She was such a gift in my life, and I owe so much to this wonderful, wise woman. Within a month of my first meeting, I had an official clean date. By the time Rocky's fourth birthday rolled around in May, I had truly begun my journey of recovery.

I attended meetings of Alcoholics Anonymous (AA) and occasionally went to Narcotics Anonymous (NA) as well. I learned so much from these people. I have been told that only one in ten people in recovery manages to stay clean and sober. Sure, there were people at the meetings who only showed up because they were court ordered to attend, but there were plenty of people who truly wanted to turn their lives around. I watched people go in and out of the programs; going out and drinking or using again, and they never came back better.

I remember riding in the car with my dad one day shortly after I got clean and sober. We were discussing recovery. He confessed to me that what hurt him the most when I was still using was that I lied to him. I was hurt, and I apologized to him. After some thought, I realized, the worst part was how much I had been lying to myself!

There are a lot of entertaining stories about the experiences of using. There was a time in every addict's life, when the drugs worked for them. Drugs eased the pain, caused euphoria and made me feel powerful. In

recovery, I found I was better off not going into too much detail giving examples of my using, because those thoughts were like triggers; they made me want it again. I still stop people today when they start to fondly reminisce about their using days. Sometimes it seems like former drunks and addicts almost brag about how bad they were. As if it were some sort of competition.

Hearing people glorify their experiences causes me to remember when it still worked for me, and that is dangerous territory for me to go to in my mind. I prefer to keep it behind me. For years after giving it all up. I had many dreams about using and drinking again. I haven't had a drinking or using dream in recent years, but when I would have them, it was usually a sign that I needed to apply some recovery in my life.

I was unable to get written permission from Alcoholics Anonymous to publish a copy of their 12 steps in this book, but they are easily found on their website (*Alcoholics Anonymous*).

Higher Power

Somehow, I managed to maintain my sobriety, but it wasn't easy. One of the things I witnessed was that people who succeeded in maintaining sobriety "worked the steps" of the program. I had a sponsor who did not allow me to shirk this difficult, but vital responsibility. The first thing I had to do was figure out a relationship with a "higher power."

Working the first step was easy. I knew I had a problem and that my life had become unmanageable. The second and third steps were not so simple. The second step tells us to believe in a power greater than ourselves and the third step suggests we turn our lives over to that power. I was still angry with God and the Jesus who I felt rejected me because of my divorce. I wasn't about to turn my life over to that power. Fortunately, AA doesn't care who your higher power is.

Although I am not Native American, I have always loved their culture and found that I could relate to the Lakota's great spirit. Putting my faith into *Wakan Tanka*, I was able to do the second step and turn myself over to a power greater than myself. This began a journey into learning about me. I was still not prepared to accept Christianity again, or any other organized religion, but I did have a spiritual reawakening, and felt a closeness with this power within me that helped me begin to restore my mind, body and spirit.

I also read Neale Donald Walsch's *Conversations with God* books early on in my recovery, and still relate strongly with his message. When I first heard about his book, I felt inexplicably drawn to it. Spice gave the first book to me for my birthday when I was just a few months into recovery. I encourage anyone seeking spiritual answers to read this series. As I read it, my spirit seemed to enigmatically soar as I felt drawn to the God that was astonishingly speaking to me through the words on the pages.

I was so grateful to have God back in my life that it made me incomprehensibly happy much of the time, especially when I was at meetings. This was called being on a "pink cloud" in the program and I know my joy irritated some people at meetings who were miserable in their struggle to get their lives back in order and to stay sober.

The fourth through eighth steps basically tell us to take a personal inventory and to learn to recognize and change things within ourselves. This is when I began to really look inside myself for the first time in my life. No more hiding from my pain and confusing feelings, and medicating myself with chemicals that helped prevent me from feeling.

Besides the cravings, I think the agony of allowing yourself to actually feel pain and emotion again is probably one of the main factors in people picking up drugs and alcohol once more. That, and hanging out with people who are still drinking and using. There is an expression that makes sense to me in why we should hang out with different people than we used or drank with, "if you hang out in a barber shop long enough, you will end up getting a haircut."

I had found such a wonderful sponsor in Spice. I remember how I would often whine or complain to her about something difficult I was experiencing, and her response would be "what is that affecting in you?" At first, of course, I would get frustrated and sometimes angry when she asked me that question, but I eventually learned to start looking inside myself. It got to the point where, when things didn't feel right for some reason, even when she wasn't around, I would hear her voice asking me "what is that affecting in you?" I would have to stop and reflect on it. I always found the answer. Understanding what it was that was affecting me helped to take away it's power.

Eventually, it wasn't Spice's voice I heard asking anymore; it was my own. Today, when I get frustrated or feel agitated, I still ask myself, "what is being affected in me?" Sometimes, it's a disagreement I had with someone (anger), an insult or criticism I received (pride), or even something as simple as a dirty look someone gave me (insecurity), or a mistake I realized I made. It's amazing how even the simplest thing could begin to change my mood. I began to have a deep understanding of how important it was (and is) to surround myself with positive people. I also learned how important it is to help others. Helping others is the best possible way to get over being hurt or in rising up out of self-pity.

The ninth and tenth steps advise us to do a personal inventory and make amends with people we have harmed. This is also the point in which many people stop working the program. When I began my journey in recovery, I truly thought I had no resentments and felt I was a victim when it came to everything I had been through. The steps helped me to not only figure out what was being affected in me, but to see another point of view when it came to the things I had been through. I was able to slowly begin to see how I had hurt others rather than just how I thought they had hurt me.

The two people I held the most resentment for were my first two husbands. The men who had taken my children away from me. I was only able to begin to forgive them after I was told I didn't have to like someone to forgive them. I still don't like Ali but I was able to see that he acted and reacted out of the only place that he understood. His culture and his own life experiences made him the way he was. This was still a very delicate place in my psyche for many years, but I always believed deep down that one day I would see my son again. That gave me a small amount of solace.

The person I realized I had the most resentment toward was Kelly. I blamed him not just for taking my kids, but for my rejection of Christianity. I blamed him for losing Luke the second time, and I blamed him for destroying our marriage. It wasn't until I worked the steps that I was able to begin to see things about myself and my behavior that I had never seen before. I was able to see my part in it and stop blaming him for everything.

I recall more than one incident during our marriage where I harbored resentment related to alcohol. I learned in AA that alcoholism is a disease.

One drink can set off a craving that is inexplicable. One time, Kelly and I went to a beautiful mountain-top restaurant in Costa Rica for our anniversary. It was an amazing place with high glass walls and absolutely beautiful decor. We ordered a glass of wine with dinner, which was a rare event, as we very seldom drank alcohol. I had one glass and wanted more. He told me no. Neither of us knew that I had activated an abnormal obsession for alcohol with that one drink; that I physically craved more. I'm sure he was thinking of the cost, and I was thinking "how dare he tell me no!" My resentment was activated. I didn't know it at the time, of course.

One of my favorite quotes, that I learned in recovery, is "resentment is like taking poison and hoping the other person dies." Once you begin to have resentment toward someone, it continues to grow unless you recognize and consciously stop it. I didn't even know I had resentment. The good news is that once you acknowledge it, you can begin to overcome it.

Another of my shortcomings is that I was never good at confrontation. When someone hurt or upset me, I would say nothing. Very early in our marriage, during an intimate moment in bed, I tried to direct his hand. He snapped at me, saying that he knew what he was doing. In my opinion, he didn't; and I never enjoyed intimacy with him after that. But I never told him.

Resentment is such a powerful force. I was good at biting my tongue and not yelling or screaming; as I had vowed when I was a little girl that I would never do; but I allowed myself to be filled with resentment without even knowing it. All three of my husbands seemed surprised and confused when I decided I had endured enough, and I wanted out of the relationship. For the most part, I didn't fight; I just left.

Working the steps helped me to recognize just how much resentment I harbored and how to begin to overcome it. The day eventually came where I was able to let go of my resentment and forgive Kelly, and even ask him to forgive me for my part in the destruction of our relationship. I don't remember what all was said, but it was the beginning of much healing. We do have a civil relationship today without resentment on my part. We were eventually even able to celebrate important events in our kids' lives together. He has gone on to be very successful and I have much respect for him.

The last two steps basically tell us to continue our relationship with

God and to share recovery with others; continuing to work the steps every day. Although I don't attend very many meetings anymore, I do continue to work the steps in my life and continue to try and be of service to others.

Today, I have a powerful relationship with God, although some of my friends and family would probably be disappointed to know I don't claim a religion. I commune with God on a regular basis and do pray for good, positive energy and healing for friends and family. I often buy meals for others in secret and give unexpected gifts and money to people when I feel impressed to do so. I meditate on what God wants from me and consider myself to be a very spiritual person.

CHAPTER 9

Fulfilling A Life-Long Dream!

Over the years, I always dreamt of going back to school someday and completing a college degree.

Once I started to get my life back together, returning to college was something I learned I could do. I worked part-time slinging burgers at a little café in a place designed for people in recovery. It is still a popular safe place where people who are trying to stay clean and sober can hang out. AA and NA meetings are held there several times a day. Other types of meetings are also held there; such as Alanon and Narcanon, which are programs to help individuals who care about alcoholics and addicts, to better cope with the actions of their loved ones. My mom says Alanon helped her a lot emotionally.

In the spring of 1998, I finally started on the journey to fulfill my lifelong dream; I enrolled at the local college. I had a wonderful advisor who helped me significantly. I truly felt she believed in me. Her encouragement was priceless. She guided me, assisted me in finding scholarships, and helped me much more than she will probably ever know.

I loved school! Sure, there were tough times and I was often tempted to give up, but I stuck with it; one day at a time. In May of 1999, I graduated

with an Associate Degree in English. Later that summer, I moved nearly 150 miles from home and enrolled at a university. Thus, I was beginning another new chapter in my life!

I also began attending AA meetings in the small university town. My social life up to this point pretty much consisted of recovery. The meetings were conducted differently, but the message was the same. At first, I was returning to my hometown every weekend. I missed my friends in recovery and when I went to meetings there, I would tell people I felt the recovery wasn't as good in the university town as it was with them. One day, while I was complaining, a man who I had known since I first began going to meetings, said to me "You're still sober aren't you?" This was another one of those dart to the heart God moments. His words went right into my heart and I realized "different doesn't mean worse." It was exactly what I needed to hear.

I returned to the meetings where I now lived with a change of attitude. I began to reach out to others, to make friends, and to stop judging the fact that some of the format of meetings was "different" than what I had become accustomed to. Funny how, when I changed my attitude, recovery there became equally as satisfying and rewarding for me as it had been before I moved.

Sunny

In 1999, Elton John was doing a benefit concert, in honor of a young man named Matthew Shepard. Matthew suffered a horrific murder when he was tortured, tied to a fence, and left to die because of his sexual orientation. It was a horrible tragedy. There is much more to be said about this sad event; please go to the Matthew Shepard Foundation to learn more (*Our Story*).

My daughter Bessie had been friends with Matthew, and I attended his funeral. The event was highly publicized as a hate crime. There were hundreds of people attending the services from across the country. While standing in the very long line waiting to go into the church, I met a young man from California who had worked as a historian in the making of the movie Titanic, which had come out a couple years earlier. He told me he was attending the funeral in honor of his own boyfriend who had been killed in a similar hate crime.

It wasn't long after Matthew's death that I was at a meeting where tickets were being distributed to the Elton John benefit concert. A very pretty young woman named Sunny was at the meeting I was attending that day. I didn't know her, but as she and I were both getting a concert ticket, we visited with each other briefly. It seemed like a good idea to go to the performance together. We were both students at the university and ended up having a wonderful evening with one another at the concert. It was the beginning of a lasting friendship. We lightheartedly joke now about being "introduced via Elton John."

Sunny and I spent much time together over the next few years of college and are still BFF's (best friends forever). Sunny grew up on an island in Alaska where her dad was a salmon fisherman. She is like the sister I never had and was also helpful with my kids and very involved in my life while we were in school.

Although we don't see one another as often as we would like, since we now live in different towns, when we do get together it's always as if no time has passed. She is one of the most beautiful people I know; inside and out. She has a heart of gold and is forever going out of her way to help others. I love her dearly.

Return of Lyle

After the first semester in student housing at the university, I felt I needed a larger place to live. I had originally moved with just Rocky, but soon found myself raising Beau as well. When he was about two, Bessie brought him to visit me along with her boyfriend at the time. They told me about Beau accidentally shooting the guy in the butt with a paintball gun after he had left it on the kitchen table. The boyfriend thought it was hilarious, but I was horrified. Bessie was still a teenager and had some wild oats to sow. I suggested she leave Beau with me and she consented. Beau is only three years younger than Rocky, so I proceeded to raise them like brothers.

During that first semester at the university, I also soon had Lyle return

full time. When he was seventeen, his dad allowed him to come live with me. He was still in his junior year and struggled to fit in at the local high school. He had previously attended a Christian school in Colorado and had no friends where we were now residing.

I personally believe that the social aspect of high school is very valuable for young people, but in Lyle's case, we decided it would be in his best interest to try and get his General Education Diploma. He aced the tests with high scores and received his high school diploma within a few weeks. Besides the closeness that he and I had always shared, Lyle was a huge help with Rocky and Beau. Lyle and Rocky continue to have a very strong bond. Lyle has always been a considerate, caring man and today is the father of two wonderful little girls. I am very proud of the man he has become.

Shortly after Lyle came to live with me, we began to look for a larger place to live. My brother Joe soon joined the household as well.

Joe

In 1984, when I was pregnant with Theo, I had a dream about my brother, Joe. It was a strange dream, indeed. It was Joe in the dream; yet it wasn't Joe. At least not the Joe I knew. There was something very different about him and I didn't understand it at the time.

I used to say that my older brother thought his purpose in life was to torment me, but I suppose most big brothers are mean to their little sisters. He was my biggest bully growing up. As a young girl, he is the one who told me what a freak I was, taught me I didn't have a glass jaw when he punched me in the face, shot an arrow at me that (fortunately) stuck in the screen door instead of into me, and who tormented me mercilessly (in my opinion). He also introduced me to smoking cigarettes (which I could never tolerate) and gave me my first tastes of alcohol and marijuana.

After high school, he served four years in the U.S. Navy. Our relationship did get better when we were older, but he was much more raucous than I was. Sometime during his late twenties he left a good job and disappeared on his Harley Davidson with a wild new girlfriend. We

hadn't heard from him in a long time when I had the disturbing dream about him.

Late one night, shortly after my strange dream, the police came to Mom and Dad's door. Joe had been in a serious motorcycle accident in Texas. What a nightmare this was; especially for Mom and Dad. Joe had been drinking and doing cocaine after work and was heading to dinner with a friend. He was on his Harley, and the rear brakes were gone. He apparently thought he could make it through the yellow light before it changed, and a car coming up to the intersection saw that the light was about to turn green so didn't slow down. This was before they had the delays that lights have now, where the light is red all 4 directions for a second or so. They collided in the intersection and Joe went through their windshield.

Joe was not wearing a helmet. He was in very bad shape, suffering numerous broken bones, contusions, internal injuries and head trauma. Eventually, everything healed except his brain. Today, we refer to him as a living example of why you should wear a helmet on a motorcycle. In fact, I have since known several people who died in motorcycle crashes because they weren't wearing helmets. I've also known individuals who got up after crashing their bikes and walked away with cracked helmets. Obviously, I am an advocate for wearing these valuable, life-saving head coverings.

Mom, Dad and I rushed to Austin, Texas to be with Joe. I was 6 months pregnant with Theo at the time. To make a long story short, Joe was in a deep coma for 7 months and it took him 4 years to completely come out of the coma. This period was such a nightmare for Mom and Dad. They spent much of their time caring for him over the next few years. Since he was a veteran, he spent time in and out of veteran's hospitals and half-way houses. As a veteran, he got disability benefits which were vital financially, but he was definitely suffering from severe brain injury.

I could devote another entire book to Joe and all his experiences. *Needless to say, the dream I had before his accident depicted him as he is now.* Joe's vision was impaired, and one hand was left deformed; all results of the brain injury. He had balance issues that made walking difficult. He had (and has) anger issues; which are typical with brain injury, but overall Joe has a generous nature. He is kind of like *"Rain Man"* in the movie with Dustin Hoffman and Tom Cruise when it comes to money.

Joe lost all memory of his life before the accident, but he always knows exactly how much cash he has on him. I have witnessed him go off in anger yelling at a cashier who accidentally shorted him a couple cents when counting out his change. To say he loves money is an understatement. As family, we always had fun trying to come up with original ways to give him money for his birthday and Christmas. All he ever wants is money, so we have always tried to be creative in coming up with new ways to give it to him.

If we gave him a shirt, we put a few dollars in each pocket. If I gave him a box of candy or a can of snacks, I taped money to it. Once, I got helium balloons and tied money to the ribbons so that when he opened the box, money floated out with the colorful balloons. My brother Ralph once gave Joe a gag "can of nuts" that had a spring-operated foam snake inside instead of real peanuts. When you opened it, the snake sprang out of the can. Ralph stuffed one-dollar bills around the snake so when Joe opened the container, all he saw was money flying everywhere. We were all entertained as he scrambled around gathering up all the bills. Joe loved it!

Joe wanted his independence, but he also loved gambling, playing bingo and, unfortunately, panhandling. We needed to monitor his behavior when he was out in public. More than once, the police brought him home. One time it was for hanging out at an ATM. He had been asking people for "a little help" as he saw them take cash from the machine. People called the police on him.

Another time, he had gone to the bowling alley and had a beer. When he was walking home, police stopped him. They saw his stagger (from his disabilities) and smelled his breath. They arrested him for public intoxication. He wasn't drunk, he was suffering brain injury and didn't walk normally, but they didn't know that. They kept him overnight and he ended up spending it in their infirmary, which turned out to be a bad experience for them due to his incapacities. After that night, whenever the police picked him up, they would just bring him home. It didn't happen frequently, but often enough to make a note of it.

Once, I had a friend who was a roofer tell me he saw my brother from the rooftop, carrying a sweater door to door trying to sell it. I had no idea where the sweater came from. Joe moved back and forth between living with me, with our parents, veterans' centers and facilities for brain injury

victims. Unfortunately, he often got kicked out of places for his erratic behavior. One time in a home for veterans, another guy convinced Rob to sneak in and steal their neighbor's bank card. Unable to use it, because they didn't have the security code, they got caught sneaking back in to return the card and were kicked out of the facility.

At different points in my recovery, I had Joe living with me. He was a lot of work for me and for my kids, but his disability check helped to pay the rent. It made sense, after I had moved for college, that I would take him in again. Between the help of his disability check, my part-time work, and my financial aid, we were able to move into a small five-bedroom, 2-bathroom house within an hour's walking distance from the university.

After I brought Joe to live with me, the first thing I did was take him to the local police department to introduce him. Between my going to classes, my recovery, and caring for the boys, there's no way Joe was going to stay home alone all day and I wanted to make sure the local police knew who he was.

One Halloween he dressed up as a pirate. The police brought him home because he had been scaring people (unintentionally) as he tried to trick-or-treat in the middle of the day. He was a big, gruff-looking biker-type guy with a patch on his eye and a plastic hook for a hand asking for handouts. If I hadn't known him, I probably would've been frightened too!

Joe did pretty well over the next couple years living with me, but it was definitely a challenge. He got a ticket once for peeing in the alley behind our house. The neighbors saw him and called the police. I had to take him to court along with a statement from his doctor proving he has a condition where his brain doesn't give him much notice when he needs to urinate. He had to be hooked up to a condom catheter at night or he would soak the bed. He frequently got kicked out of places for panhandling or making messes (usually in the bathroom), but most people accepted him once they realized his disabilities. He loved his independence, and there was no way I could make him stay home alone all day. He was always on the go.

A department store once gave him a credit card, which was ridiculous. I don't know how he was able to get it since he wasn't able to write well enough to fill out an application, but we found out about it when he got a huge credit card bill. Mom and Dad took care of it and warned him about not trying something like that again.

Mom was his official payee. His Social Security pension checks were deposited into her account and she then sent me a check to cover his portion of the rent, and funds from which I purchased cigarettes and gave Joe an allowance each day. His biggest expense was cigarettes. He wasn't allowed to smoke inside, and was given one pack at a time, which helped to control his behavior. (I think he found "friends" to help him use up his smokes and money).

One time, we discovered the television from his bedroom in the basement was missing. He confessed that he had pawned it. I have no idea how he could have taken the heavy screened box to the pawn shop without help considering he could only use one arm. This was before the new lightweight flat-screen televisions! Dad was visiting when we realized it was missing and he promptly took Joe to the pawn shop where he lectured them about dealing with an obviously mentally challenged man.

In early spring of 2002, before I graduated from the university, we had a typical cold, snowy day. Before I left for classes I told Joe to stay home since it was icy outside and he could not walk well. He didn't listen to me. Later that morning I received a call as his emergency contact. He had decided to take himself out for lunch. Walking down the street, he slipped and fell on a patch of ice and broke his hip. This was the beginning of a long period of rehabilitation and change of lifestyle for Joe. After a brief stay in the hospital, and then a local nursing home, Mom and Dad returned him to their town, where he spent several months in an assisted living facility. Thankfully, he had veteran's benefits and Medicaid.

Eventually, he was placed in a halfway house for brain injury victims. He has received full time care since then; even having his own assisted living apartment. After living in our town for a few years, the local offices shut down. Joe was moved to another facility run by the same organization in a town 120 miles from where Mom and Dad lived, where he remains to this day. I am his payee now, and I mail monthly rent and allowance checks to the facility where he lives. They pay his general bills, distribute his daily pocket money to him, monitor his activities, and oversee his medical care. He uses a wheelchair now to get around, so is much less mobile.

Joe loves the fact that there is a tribal casino in the town where he now lives, and he is rewarded for good behavior by getting to make trips to gamble. Joe was diagnosed with COPD a few years ago and quit smoking

so has more money to spend, which is very convenient for him considering how much he loves slot machines. I still visit him regularly and bring him home for holidays and special occasions.

College Life

From 2000 to 2002, I was a very busy woman. I was attending college full-time, remaining active in recovery, taking care of my disabled brother, and raising my two boys and grandson. By this time, I had found a good local doctor, was treating my diabetes, and was back on insulin.

We got a new puppy who was a black lab, golden retriever mix, and Rocky named her Mysterious. We called her "Mysti" for short. We fell in love with her. I wanted her to be a good car dog, so took her for a ride every day. It took 30 days before she stopped crying in the car, and after that, we could take her anywhere. She was an amazing part of our family for the next thirteen years. She was, by far, the best dog I ever owned.

I became a participant of the McNair Scholars Program, which is a TRIO program designed to help disadvantaged students prepare for graduate school. The McNair Program was started by the family of Dr. Ronald McNair, one of the scientists who died when the space shuttle Challenger exploded in 1986 (*About Ronald E. McNair, Ph.D.*).

I did a research project while I was in McNair entitled *"Reasons Why Children Are Being Raised by Their Grandparents; From the Grandparent Perspective"*. When I was struggling to decide on a topic for my research, I realized that I could base my work on my own personal experience as a grandparent raising her grandson. I composed a survey and distributed it locally. I did a lot of research. I loved being in the program and met some of the most supportive people I have ever known while in it. I got to travel to different universities to present my findings.

I was presenting in New York one time, and afterwards learned that Dr. Ronald McNair's brother was in the audience. He commented on my presentation to my mentor. She told me that Mr. McNair said I did a wonderful presentation. He went on to roll his eyes and added, "and believe me I see a lot of them!" That boosted my self-confidence!

My two McNair mentors were (and are) wonderful women. Whenever anyone has ever asked me if there has been an influential person in my life that inspired me, I always think of them. I dearly love, respect and admire them to this day!

The results of my research (which was published in a McNair publication), showed that the number one reason for children being raised by their grandparents is drug and alcohol use by the parent. In my own case, it was the young age of the parent at the grandchild's birth; which I found to be the second most common reason.

My only regret with McNair is that I did not continue my education and get a PhD, which is their objective. Honestly though, I don't know if I could have even achieved my bachelor's degree without the encouragement and assistance that I received from the McNair Scholars Program. I am forever grateful. (*Little did I know then that TRIO programs would continue to have great impact on my life in the future*).

While at the university, I went back and forth in deciding on a major for my degree, which is common for many college students. I discovered I could design my own degree through what is called a distributed major. In 2002, I received a bachelor's degree in Humanities. This consisted of English, Spanish, and Women's Studies with emphasis in Social Work and Counseling; all of which were my major at one point or another. I also did a semester of secondary education. I learned a lot and I like to think my degree at least makes me sound like a well-rounded individual!

Going to school while caring for my brother and the boys was often very challenging. I remember times after a big exam when, as we were leaving the building, my classmates would all be talking about how much they deserved a drink now! I had to resist the thought that I deserved one, too! I had to find ways to make myself feel better without having that drink.

First of all, I needed to "think it through" and know that one drink would just make my life worse. Another great saying in AA is "one drink is too many and a thousand is never enough." Meaning that one drink just sets the craving for more into motion.

Some of the things that helped me through those bouts of temptation were to eat an ice cream, go to a meeting where I could talk about it with people who understood, go for a swim, take a bubble bath, do a fun game or puzzle, etc. My favorite, when I could afford it, was to go to a movie. I

could take my mind off everything that was going on in my life for two hours! It was a great reprieve and I always felt better afterwards. I still try to get away and go to movies by myself; not just as an escape, but because I enjoy them. Of course, I love movie popcorn.

I believe it is invaluable to find little ways to reward yourself in life; even if it only makes you feel slightly better. Once I start to feel bad, I have a choice. I can dwell on it and continue to spiral downward, or I can do something to change how I feel. Even the slightest turn towards something positive, improves how I think and begins to lead me in a better direction.

I met with a family support therapist for a while when I was in college and she was incredibly encouraging and helpful. I dearly appreciated and valued her. Today, I am a strong advocate for counseling and therapy. Many times, people have told me they didn't believe in counseling because they tried it once and didn't like their therapist. I encourage them to find someone else, then. Finding someone you can talk to can make a tremendous difference in your life, but it is vital to find someone you feel you can relate to. Keep trying and don't give up.

CHAPTER 10

Return To My Hometown

After fulfilling my life-long dream of getting my bachelor's degree, I was faced with another huge life change. Not knowing what to do or where to go, the next logical step was to return home.

I finished up my degree in 2002 and returned to my home town. Rocky, Beau and I moved in with Mom & Dad while I started looking for work. I went to a temp agency and took all their placement tests. I scored so highly they hired me to work full-time for their organization. I enjoyed the work, but also continued job hunting.

Before that summer ended, I accepted two job offers. One was as an adjunct Spanish instructor at the local college. I started teaching evening classes during the fall semester and loved it. I was also offered a secretarial position with the city municipality. I had been a secretary before getting my degree so had lots of administrative experience. I didn't need a degree for the job but was told by my new boss that having a degree did help in me being the one selected for the position.

I remember the final "interview" for the position was to attend a pot luck dinner at the manager's house along with the other candidates and

people I would be working with. This seemed unusual to me, but I decided to just relax and be myself. I got along well with everyone, had a good time, and I got the job! The position came with benefits, and I couldn't turn it down. I very much admired my boss; a remarkable, supportive woman.

I thoroughly enjoyed teaching Spanish at the college and taught evening classes there for five years. The first semester, one of my students was a physician who I began seeing for my diabetes. He introduced me to the insulin pump which made a huge difference in my diabetes control. It was wonderful not having to stick myself with needles numerous times per day. I remained on the pump for many years and it helped tremendously with maintaining control of my blood sugars.

I met many interesting people while teaching Spanish. One thing I can say about teaching evening classes is that most of the students were older "non-traditional" students who were there because they wanted to be; not because they had to be. During the five years I taught Spanish at the college, I always had a dinner at my favorite Mexican restaurant, as part of the final exam. All students were invited. For those who couldn't afford to eat out, I always had other students who would pitch in to help me pay (anonymously on both sides). Students weren't graded on the dinner other than participation points, but the servers spoke Spanish and it gave the students the opportunity to use some of what they had learned. I required each student to place their order in Spanish and the servers worked with me. These dinners were always popular, and I still eat there regularly and enjoy being able to use my Spanish.

After a couple years working as a secretary for the city, I applied for an Administrative Assistant position in another department and was selected. This was a raise in pay, and I was now working for the Public Utilities manager. Among other duties, I took minutes for several municipal board meetings and learned much about serving on a Board of Directors. I also served on the local college Alumni Association Board of Directors for a while. I was still very involved in recovery and soon served on the Board of Directors at the previously mentioned recovery center.

Many people in recovery still have relationships with people who drink, but it never worked out for me. I tried dating guys who drank, but inevitably, while they were drinking, they wanted to come see me.

Kissing a man with alcohol on his breath didn't gross me out. It was

worse than that – it tasted good and made me want a drink. So, early on in my recovery I chose not to date or hang out with people who drank. It's not that I was judging anyone else for their choices or decisions, but it worked for me and made my recovery easier. I also sponsored numerous people in the program and continued to attend regular meetings. I like to say, I had to do more than "work" the 12 steps; I had to "live" them.

Haunted House

Shortly after I returned to our hometown and began working full time, I moved into a very old house with Rocky and Beau. Of course, Mysti moved with us. Lyle had met a gal on-line in Ohio and moved out there to be with her. We liked the house, but it was definitely haunted. The lights would flicker, and I could feel a strange presence. Once, cans flew off a shelf, almost hitting one of my little boys as they walked past it.

Some friends and I did a smudge of the house, with burning sage, and I "had a talk" with whoever the presence was. I sensed it was a woman and I acknowledged to the unknown entity that she was there first and I was the trespasser. Basically, I asked that we be able to share the house. Afterwards, all the light flickering and can flying stopped and my sense of unease dissipated.

There was still one room in the far end of the basement that was extremely uncomfortable, though. At one point, when Rocky was about nine, he decided he wanted his own space. He didn't want to share a room with Beau anymore and since the downstairs room was vacant, he asked if it could be his bedroom. We moved a bed and a few of his things down there. He spent one night in the room and, although he couldn't seem to express why, he refused to go into the room again. I moved his things back upstairs and we stopped going into that room; avoiding it as much as possible.

Not long after I returned, Bessie decided she was ready to take Beau back. I was reluctant to give him up, but I knew what it was like to not be with your son. She had a new boyfriend who was full of promises about their future together. He also had two children that were close to Beau's age. I didn't know why, but the guy gave me the creeps and I never liked

him. I told myself that God gave Beau to Bessie though, so when he was almost six years old, he left with his mom and they moved to Mississippi.

Living with My Parents

Later that year Mom, Dad and I decided to buy a house together. They were renting a house several miles from mine, and we spent much time going back and forth between my house and theirs for babysitting, etc. We had so much fun looking at houses! In late Spring of 2003, we found a five-bedroom, two-bathroom brick house that seemed perfect for us. It wasn't in the best neighborhood, but that made it more affordable.

Mom and Dad's names were on the mortgage, and we put all the utilities in my name. They lived on the main floor and Rocky and I lived in the three-bedroom basement, to which we soon added a kitchen. The arrangement worked well for us. We had separate entrances but there was an enclosed foyer where Rocky (and the dogs) could easily go back and forth between the two residences. This was ideal since I had two jobs and my parents watched Rocky while I taught in the evenings and attended meetings. We shared household responsibilities and got along well. We did most of our meals together, while still maintaining our privacy. We continued to live there together until my father's death in 2014.

Another Ghost!

I have another "ghost" story about this house. I often sensed a presence in the basement where we now lived and would hear strange noises, but since I was never afraid of ghosts, I didn't give it much thought. However, one time after Rocky had left home for college; we had an incident that was pretty freaky.

While in college, Rocky had been dating a beautiful girl whose father is a movie producer and director originally from Uruguay. She attended the same university as Rocky for a year and was returning to California where her father lived. She and Rocky decided to part as friends, and when her

father came to move her home, I invited them over for a casual dinner as they were driving through our town.

We had a lovely visit and were sitting in the living room chatting when the topic of ghosts came up. I told them about sensing a presence in this house and about the ghost in the house Rocky and I had previously lived in and they shared their own family ghost stories. Her father was finishing up a tale telling us about working on location for a film he had directed about a haunted ship. He shared his experience of searching and waiting for signs of ghosts to appear in the hull of the abandoned ship. He went on to tell us, "And… nothing happened at all. No ghosts whatsoever. So… there you have it. Ghosts are not real!"

No kidding, at that EXACT moment, a folding table that had been leaning against the wall in an "A" formation in the hallway for years, flipped over and loudly crashed! Our adrenalin was soaring! He said he never would have believed it if he hadn't seen it for himself! *We are friends on Facebook now, and I asked him if he wanted to add to my story.*

"Yes, it did happen exactly the way she has described it," he said. "I saw it! I can assure you, scientifically speaking, that if for some reason that folding table was going to suddenly fall to the floor the way it did, it would've been only by an earthquake or someone pushing it. I told those present what happened from my point of view; what I saw with my own eyes. My first…real, but totally unexplained, ghost sighting!"

Dale

It was at a meeting of Alcoholics Anonymous that I first met Dale. He was a cute guy with a long, blonde mullet and very blue eyes, which were what first attracted me to him. He had just gotten out of prison, after serving five years as a "felon with a firearm." I won't go into Dale's story too much, but to make a long story short, he had once beaten up a guy for molesting a kid. It turned out that the guy he beat up was the Sheriff's son and Dale got a felony abuse charge. Not that he was a saint; from the stories I have heard, he was a wild man.

He grew up in the same small town where I had lived for four years when I was a teen, so that was one of our first topics of conversation. I

didn't remember him from my time living there, because I am a few years older, but we knew a lot of the same people.

He dropped out of school in the eighth grade and, according to him, did a lot of drinking and drugging as a teenager. His father died of emphysema while he was still a teen. At the age of eighteen, he was sitting in a bar when someone came in and asked if anyone wanted a job as a roughneck at an oil rig.

Thus, he began his career in the oilfield. He lived a rather intense life the next few years. He married a bartender with three kids, and did more than his share of drinking, using and dealing drugs. There was a lot of drug use in the oilfields back in the day. For one thing, he tells me it was hard to work for several days non-stop without drugs to help keep you awake. It was a rough life, and he was (and still is) a very hard worker.

At this point in Dale's life, the local police and federal narcotics officers had been trying hard to catch him doing something illegal, when he and his buddy were pulled over one night. Guns were found in the vehicle and since he was a felon, he was arrested. They tried to get him to turn over information on other people, and when he refused, he was sentenced to the maximum penalty for a felon with a firearm; five years in the federal penitentiary.

Those five years were challenging for him, to say the least. His wife divorced him, his family abandoned him, and his mother died. He was unable to attend her funeral due to the cost. After a difficult period of being very poor and making do with only the essentials in prison, he inherited some money from an uncle he barely knew. Ironically, he heard from his brother again, but only because he and his wife wanted Dale to give them Power of Attorney over his finances. He turned them down. While he does have contact with his brother and sister today, their relationships are strained.

Dale tells me that the five-year sentence was the best thing that happened to him in the long run. He decided, during that difficult time, to get clean and sober. He says there are plenty of ways to get high and/or drunk in the penitentiary, but he decided it wasn't worth it. He joined a Christian running group, got his high school equivalency degree, and made a conscious decision to turn his life around. He got truly clean and sober for the first time since he was fourteen years old.

Papas with Ponytails

When he got out of prison, he was placed in a community re-entry center and vowed he would never marry again. He got a job, and started attending AA meetings, where he met me. I was casually dating another guy at the time, but really liked Dale. I went through a brief period where I didn't know which guy would be the right one for me. I wasn't sleeping with either one. After knowing each other for a couple months though, Dale and I kissed for the first time and my choice was made.

My parents, and even my sponsor, were mortified when I began dating Dale exclusively. He was an ex-con! I felt I saw him for who he was now; a kind, gentle, hardworking man who was rough around the edges, but clean and sober and working on his recovery. They saw him for where he came from and were pretty concerned for a while. I can honestly say, I don't believe Dale and I would have gotten along if we were still drinking and/or using, but we had both turned our lives around. Recovery was, and is, our greatest common denominator.

I helped Dale find a place to live when he got out of the halfway house and we dated for many years before he moved in with me. Meanwhile, he won my parents over. He was very handy to have around, as he could fix anything and was happy to do so. Dale went through a lot before he became the man I now know.

Rocky was eleven when Dale and I first got together, and although his gruff exterior scared Rocky at first, that soon changed. While I was still going to college, Rocky's legal dad had stopped contact with him, which was difficult for Rocky. However, Rocky now had both Papa and Dale around to help serve as father figures. Rocky and Dale developed a strong bond that they still share.

Dale and I have been together longer than I have been with any other man, although we never married. We are both quite independent and while we are devoted to each other, we give one another plenty of space. He is good to my kids, and I must give him kudos for always "holding down the fort" since I travel so much. My grandkids refer to him as "Papa Dale" and he does have a ponytail!

Alexandra Flowers

My Parenting Style

I never liked the idea of spanking (or hitting) a child. I believe hands are for loving. Rocky was always a great kid. He had normal growing up issues being from a divorced family and a year or so with a messed-up mother, but overall was an awesome boy. Once, when he was only about three, he was throwing a temper tantrum. I drew a picture depicting what he looked like with spit and tears spurting from his mouth and eyes and taped the drawing on his door showing him what he looked like when he threw a fit. He studied that picture…and never threw a tantrum like that again. Not that he never cried or showed emotions, but he stopped throwing tantrums.

There were rare occasions, when he was very young, that I did try spanking him, but it only made the situation worse. I never responded well to spankings when I was a child. In fact, I remember one spanking I received where I ran and hid under my bed afterwards; praying that I would die and that my mom would find me dead and regret hitting me. I don't at all remember what the spanking was for.

I soon learned that discussions and rewards worked better with Rocky than physical punishment, which went along well with my values. He learned there are consequences for your actions, but Mom is there for loving and guiding; not for hitting and screaming.

When he was in first grade, he rode the bus to school. We were waiting patiently at the bus stop when the bus pulled up. Suddenly, little Rocky burst into tears and took off running towards home. I was shocked and ran after him. I asked what was wrong and he confessed to me that a big girl on the bus had been hurting him. I took him to school and the bullying issue was dealt with, but he told me later, "Mommy, I'm the goodest boy at school, and the baddest boy at home." I thought that was very sweet and said, "well, I guess that's better than the other way around." But really, he was never a bad boy at home either, and was always a loving, considerate and intelligent boy. (Except when he saw a spider. He wasn't afraid of them, but he knew I didn't like them so when he saw one, especially as a teenager, he would leave it for me to find and then laugh when I yelped upon discovering it).

I did get a call from the police one time when Rocky was a teenager.

Papas with Ponytails

He had gone to a birthday party where alcohol was being served to minors. Rocky didn't like the taste and went to a back room to lay down after only a couple sips. He was awakened by a police flashlight being shined in his face. I was told I was the only parent who was called to come pick up their child. All the other kids were taken to jail. Rocky's blood alcohol level proved he hadn't been drinking. Rocky was always pretty level headed and even tempered, while still being fun and charming.

Rocky did Reserve Officers' Training Corps (ROTC) in high school and became a staff member. He was very self-disciplined and had a strong sense of what is right. Rocky also had beautiful hair. His long light brown curls were down to his shoulders by the time he was fifteen. When he first joined ROTC, he was told he had to cut it off. He felt it was discriminating that boys had to cut their hair short, but girls did not. He brought his issue to the higher-ups and apparently made a reasonable argument. They conceded and told him he just needed to keep his hair above his collar line.

Rocky then proceeded to get a "faux-hawk" (a fake mohawk). Every morning he got up and worked his hair over with lots of hairspray and gel so that all his hair stood up and did not touch his collar. He did this for a few weeks, but soon decided it was far too time-consuming. He broke down and cut his hair.

He did well in ROTC and received several awards and commendations. He always maintained excellent grades and earned good scholarships. He also enjoyed being a part of the ROTC Color Guard. Papa was very proud of Rocky. I remember Papa gazing at Rocky wearing his ROTC uniform, with tears in his eyes as he beamed with pride. Rocky still enjoys dressing up and loves wearing a suit.

We survived high school, and Rocky graduated in 2011. During his senior year, he applied for the Air Force National Guard, which he planned to participate in while attending college. Unfortunately, he was turned down because of a small patch of eczema on his forearm. He was quite disappointed. He had attended Naval Summer Academy in 2010 but was only interested in the Air Force.

He was accepted to several universities and chose to attend the university that offered him the best scholarships. Like me, he discovered he has an affinity for vernaculars, and he studied languages, philosophy and International Studies. He spent a summer in China and a whole semester

studying Russian and teaching English in Russia. Rocky earned a double major in International Studies and Russian with a minor in Mandarin.

He made the Russian newspaper while he was in Russia. Walking home from class one day, he witnessed an elderly man get struck by a car and he rushed over to help. Rocky was surprised that no-one else came to the man's aid. He stayed with the man until the police and the man's family arrived. The news article described the "young American student" as helpful and pleasant but expressed surprise at his caring actions. We were very proud of him at home, though. In fact, his professor and advisor at the university he was enrolled in is the person who told me about Rocky's act of kindness. I felt it showed what kind of young man I had raised.

CHAPTER 11

Papa

I was always a "daddy's girl." I loved and adored my dad more than any other man I have ever known.

Papa and I had two huge things in common; diabetes and recovery from alcoholism. We had a wonderful relationship and, as I stated previously, I was very much a daddy's girl. My dad was fun-loving, kind, generous, creative, and always the life of the party. Above all, he adored his grandchildren. They were the most important people in his life. They referred to him as Papa, and soon all our friends and family called him Papa. He was such an amazing man, and everyone loved and adored him. He was born on 10/20/30 and was very proud of his birth date, which he often told people.

Papa had a fantastic sense of humor and loved to joke and tease. He especially loved to tease Mama (or Grammy as my kids call her). Of course, she reacted just the way he wanted her to. For example, we were eating out one night, and he had ordered a salad in a bread bowl. His eyes sparkled as he picked up the bread bowl and announced, "this could be my new hat!" As he proceeded to lift it up towards his head, he looked at Mama with anticipation. Sure enough, before he got it on his head, she exclaimed, "Papa! Don't you dare!" We all laughed, as we knew his game! My sons have always been attracted to girls they can tease the same way Papa teased Grammy.

Papa had adored his first grandchild. He played with little Luke every

chance he got. I chuckle when I think about the time 2-year-old Luke was feeding Papa pieces of his fruit roll-up. Papa was happily playing with Luke, making smacking noises and causing lots of laughter and giggles. That is, until he turned the fruit strip over and saw that it was covered with dog hair, dirt and fuzz. You should have seen the look of shock and disgust on Papa's face! On a serious note, though; Papa, like the rest of us, was heartbroken when Luke was taken.

Papa had also attended AA for a while and stopped drinking alcohol completely when Bessie was pretty young. He was always very involved in his grandchildren's lives. I'm proud that my kids never knew Papa as a drinker.

Papa referred to Bessie, his first (and only) granddaughter as his little darling and she inherited his green thumb. They were always close to each other, and she loved spending time in his garden with him. One time I gave Papa a block of his favorite Blue Cheese for Christmas. I later found my little one-year-old Bessie sitting on his lap eating the stinky stuff with him. She smelled like fermented cheese for days, despite many baths. (*Is it any wonder she still loves the stuff*)?

Papa had cute nicknames for all my kids. When Lyle was born, Papa says that, as he gazed into Lyle's big blue eyes, the baby gurgled little bird-like sounds, "hooo, hooo." After that, Papa always referred to Lyle as his little "hooter." They always had a special bond. Theo was dubbed "Peanut." Theo was a very bright little boy, and always delighted Papa. Papa taught the boys to fish and often worked on projects with them.

Papa was an avid gardener. For as long as I can remember we always had fresh vegetables from his garden. We didn't have a long growing season due to the harsh cold winter weather, but he made the most of our limited summers. I was forever grateful for the love of vegetables he instilled in my children. I can remember them throwing down their lollipops at Grammy & Papa's house in order to eat a fresh carrot from Papa's garden!

A few years after we bought the house together, Mama began spending winters in Arizona working flea markets with my brother Ralph. Papa went with her one year, but he felt the nights were too cold. We always laughed about Papa thinking Arizona was too cold. After that, he stayed home with Dale, Rocky and I during the winter months. We spent a lot of time together and the four of us were all very devoted to one another. Papa and

Dale both loved going to the casino and we made frequent trips. I didn't go as often as Dale and Papa did, and they became fast friends.

Someday I would love to write a book full of Papa's anecdotes because I know it would be very entertaining. Papa collected frog knick-knacks for years, so we always associate frogs with Papa. Of course, if I mention Papa's love of frog knickknacks, I should tell you about my mom's giraffe collection. She literally has thousands of giraffes! I was at a hobby store one time and told an acquaintance I ran into that I was looking for a giraffe to give my mom. The person proceeded to tell me where all they had seen giraffes. I stopped them and said, "let me rephrase that; I'm looking for a giraffe that she doesn't already have!" Papa always managed to find unique giraffes for her.

He used to joke around that our ancestors must have been starving, because we love food so much! He enjoyed cooking and always had dinner waiting for us when we came home from work. Granted, sometimes he had made it two or three hours earlier in the day, but at least he made it. One time we came home to find he had made meatloaf for everyone. He announced proudly, "I made one loaf with bacon and one with nuts and raisins since you all liked it so much last time!" The raisin meatloaf did get eaten, although we were slightly confused. After I gave it some thought, I told him later, "Papa, I think that was when you made zucchini bread."

Not one to waste food, he once made a rice dish out of hamburger that had been in the refrigerator too long. I went upstairs to see what the horrible smell was, and he tried to get me to sample it. The hamburger was rotten. I refused to even taste it, and later baked some cookies in his oven just to help mask the smell. He ate some of it, though…and while he didn't get violently sick, his bedroom stunk like rotten meat for three days afterwards. He must've had an iron stomach.

Papa's gardening meant spending many hours in the sun, and he developed several melanomas of skin cancer over the years. He fondly referred to his dermatologist as Dr. Freeze because the doctor would "freeze" the spots off. Sadly, in 2013 he discovered a lump in his armpit that was diagnosed as cancerous.

I went with him to the oncologist who told him he was too old for surgery to have the mass removed. Papa was almost 83. However, the doctor did recommend radiation and chemotherapy. Papa said no; he didn't want

all that, but the doctor talked him into it, making him feel guilty about leaving his family. I was witness to their conversation. Looking back, I do not understand how that doctor thought surgery to remove the lump was too much of a risk but that he would be able to endure strong chemo and radiation. Papa had excellent medical coverage, though, which I felt was the major concern of the doctor.

In my opinion, the treatments killed my father. His last year of life was miserable and he developed what we called "chemo brain" where he couldn't concentrate, would forget where he was, etc. One time, Dale mentioned that it was snowing, and Papa commented that "the snowbirds won't be very happy." He thought he was in Arizona with Mama.

Another time, when he was in the hospital, he asked Mama if she would give him $20 so he could take it downstairs to the casino. We have many similar amusing stories, but in reality, his deterioration was heartbreaking to watch.

I have the utmost admiration and respect for caretakers now, and hope I never have to go through that again. I won't go into details here, but it was a horrific year for those of us who were loving and living with him. It was enough for me to say that if I ever get cancer, I will say my goodbyes before undergoing what Papa endured. At least my last months would be happy. The treatments made him so sick and miserable; I feel they just prolonged his misery. The medical profession made hundreds of thousands of dollars on him, though. It breaks my heart that we had to sit and watch him suffer and die for over a year.

Toward the end of that year, Papa began telling us of strange visitors in the night. They would come visit him while he was in bed. Were they angels, perhaps? Delusions of his failing mind? Or maybe, being close to death, he was able to visit and commune with our house ghost.

During his last few days of mental alertness, while hospitalized, the medical staff provided someone to sit with him at night so he could be continuously monitored. One morning, she reported to me that Papa had spent the entire night telling her all about the ordeal with Luke and how important his grandchildren were to him. I didn't realize how close he actually was to the end of his life, but we did decide to call the kids to come see him.

Living in different states, it took a while for all of them to arrive. Papa

slipped into a coma the next day and never came out of it. Theo and his lovely wife are the only grandkids who made it before he passed. They had their new little baby girl with them, who was just a few months old, but he was already comatose by the time they arrived. In retrospect, I don't think Papa wanted his grandchildren to see him the way he was at the end. It may sound cold-hearted, but I thought he looked better at the viewing in the mortuary than he had looked in months.

Dale had become Papa's best friend over the years, and the night before he went into the coma, after I stepped out of the room to talk to the doctor, Papa asked Dale to look after all of us, and basically said goodbye. I didn't realize the coma meant he only had hours to live, but I guess I was in denial. I had never witnessed the dying process before.

Dale had gone to work at a rig out of town the next day, thinking we still had some time. At the moment of Papa's death, a big dog came running up to Dale in the middle of nowhere and greeted him with joy and delight. Dale sensed it was Papa letting him know his time had come. After greeting the dog and calling him Papa, the dog bounded away, stopping briefly to turn around and wag his tail once more at Dale.

I have heard theories of newly departed souls choosing an animal as their spiritual transport, and Papa was an avid dog lover. I could see him choosing a dog. Who knows if it was really Papa or not; I'm sure many will scoff, but it made us feel better to think that Papa was finally out of pain and running up to his best friend with endless energy to say goodbye. I know several similar stories from family members of when their loved ones passed. My aunts think of my grandma when they have butterflies land on them, and I have cousins who believe their mom visits them in the form of hummingbirds.

Mama, Gene, Theo and I were all in the room with Papa when he took his last breath. Luke, Bessie, Lyle, and Rocky all arrived with their families within the next day to say goodbye and were a great comfort to Mama and me. In fact, that is the last time I have had all 5 of my kids together at once. The end of a legend, but his legacy continues. We love you, Papa.

One of Papa's dreams was to someday visit Australia. He never made it, but I would love to go for him one day. (*Maybe I can meet my favorite Aussie actor, Chris Hemsworth and his Spanish wife Elsa Pataky, while I'm there*).

Papa was also an avid Colorado Rockies fan. He never missed one of

their televised baseball games. About six months before he died, Theo and his wife bought us tickets, and I took Papa to Colorado. He was thrilled to be attending his first live Rockies game. I had made him a colorful poster that said, "This is on my bucket list!" Being in a wheelchair and on oxygen, while holding his big sign, he was spotted by cameramen. The media host and crew came to greet him. They gave him a Rockies t-shirt and hat. Mama, and one of my cousins who was always close to Papa growing up, got to see him on television. It was a fantastic day for Papa!

We've had lots of amazing dogs over the years, but another of Papa's dreams was to someday own a bulldog. A couple years ago, Dale adopted a pedigreed Olde English Bulldog, and we named him after Papa. Papa would have been proud!

Mama, who had been spending most of her winters in Arizona, could not afford their house without Papa's retirement income. The house needed a lot of work and it would have taken weeks, maybe even months, and lots of money, before it would be in good enough condition to be put on the market for a profit. Dale ended up buying the house from Mama as is, so she didn't have to go through a long, drawn-out process. Mama then bought a small place in Arizona where she moved to live full time with her beloved poochie (poodle chihuahua mix). She loves it there and has many friends. Dale and I moved upstairs and still live in the house. We have been slowly fixing it up and my cousin Gene rents a room in the basement. We keep a room for Mama for when she visits.

Ralph

This might be a good place to add an update on my younger brother. As I related earlier, Ralph and I were very close when we were young. Ralph is an avid hunter and fisherman and is very much a dog lover.

He has been self-employed for most of his adult life. He buys and sells antiques, rocks, and more. He is an auctioneer and has had various shops and auctions over the years. He spends half the year in Arizona. The entire town becomes a giant flea market during the winter months. Mama and my aunt join him every winter and work with him in his shops. He frequently holds auctions, and he loves what he does!

Papas with Ponytails

Mama comes from a large family with whom she is very close. Most of her six sisters come visit her in Arizona for a few weeks every winter, and I love it when I can crash their "sisters' reunions." They are all beautiful, loving women whom I treasure! I could write another whole book on her family and history. Mama is very popular in her community and has always been well-loved by everyone who knows her! She and Ralph are business partners and are very close.

CHAPTER 12

Upward Bound

Working with Teens

I saw a survey on TV once that asked whether people would prefer being stranded with a horde of zombies or with a group of teenagers. I was shocked that over 90 percent said they preferred the zombies! Not me! The key to teenagers, in my opinion, is to just regard them as people. Listen to them and treat them with respect and positivity. I actually enjoy teenagers and have always gotten along well with them.

I worked for the city for about five years when I was offered a position at the state university, working at the local campus. I received a call from someone asking me to apply for the job even though I wasn't actively job hunting. I was excited to be in a position where I would actually be using my degree.

I previously mentioned participating in the McNair Scholars Program, which I was a participant of while I was in college. McNair is one of several federal TRIO college prep programs. These Department of Education funded TRIO projects include the Upward Bound and Upward Bound Math Science programs that I went to work for in 2007. They are designed to help high school students prepare for college. Let me give you a little

history on TRIO programs based on what I learned working with them for twelve years.

In 1964, Senator Pell and President Johnson instated a grant to help low-income citizens afford college. The Pell Grant is still popular today. At that time, President Johnson recognized that people would need more than just financial assistance to succeed in college, so TRIO programs were established. These are programs that help low-income and/or first-generation students (meaning their parents don't have a four-year college degree) enter and succeed in college. Upward Bound was the first of three programs and while there are more than three programs now, the term TRIO stuck.

The Upward Bound (UB) and Upward Bound Math Science (UBMS) grants are managed by different colleges and universities throughout the United States. These programs work specifically with high school students, preparing them for college. Eligibility for the programs is based on the income of parents or guardians. Let's face it, college is expensive. Unless your parents are wealthy, the average person cannot afford to go without assistance.

Admission to college is also complicated with all the paperwork and other requirements involved. If parents don't have their own experience to fall back on, they usually have difficulty helping their children get into college. There are school counselors out there to help, but many schools are understaffed. Too many students do not get the assistance and encouragement they need. This is where TRIO programs come in.

The Council for Opportunity in Education (COE) lobbies full-time in Washington DC to help support TRIO programs around the United States. A quick internet search on the COE website, or checking with your local higher education institutions, will help you find more information about TRIO programs that may be available in your area.

As Upward Bound Project Coordinator, I was the only locally located full-time staff person and I met with students regularly. Every year I also hired part-time tutors to work with me. They were usually young college students. We provided tutoring three or more times a week and held a group meeting or enrichment, twice a month. We helped students keep up their GPA (which is vital in winning scholarships), assisted with developing better study skills, and much more. If students met the monthly time

requirements and maintained a GPA of at least 2.5 (on a 4.0 scale), they could earn forty dollars each month.

We also provided a six-week college experience for our students each summer. UB and UBMS students from around the state had the opportunity to move to the university during the summer. Students took various math, science, language, computer and composition classes during this period, along with classes such as a foreign language, nutrition, leadership and yearbook.

The main focus was to write a research paper on a topic of their choice. Students were able to pick their mentorship and were divided into teams. These mentorships included fields such as Astronomy, Forest Management, Global Terrorism, Neuroscience, Criminal Justice and more. The topics varied from summer to summer depending on who we hired as mentors that year; many of whom were PhD students.

Overall, the summer experience gave students a good taste of what college would be like. One director I worked with described the summer program as "an educational experience with a social component."

Summer program was a wonderful opportunity for students in many ways. I saw young people grow and mature significantly; especially those who attended more than one summer. I had many students be successful without attending a UB summer session, but I think it was an experience they all should have had.

I taught many courses during summer over the years including Spanish, Computer, Comp & Lit and (my favorite) Summer Yearbook. Every summer we provided a memory book for the students with photos of everyone involved and highlighting their summer activities. I enjoyed working with the students in creating these memorials.

On a personal level, however, summer program was the most difficult part of my job. I had to leave home for seven weeks (with a short break over the 4th of July). Some years I shared an apartment with a coworker and her family. While she and I got very close, it was often uncomfortable for me feeling like I was intruding on their home life. She didn't mean to make me feel that way, of course, but I did. I felt out of place living with her family and Dale wouldn't come visit when I didn't have my own place. Most years each coordinator from out of town did have their own small apartment, but there was usually a very uncomfortable bed, never any air conditioning, and sometimes even bed bugs.

I did spend most of my time with the students, which was rewarding, but summers were really difficult on a personal level. I got to where I had to try and force myself to focus on what it meant for the students and try to take myself, and my needs and comfort, completely out of the picture. That was easier said than done. Of course, there was no additional financial compensation for making these sacrifices. I made the most of it; but that was the most challenging part of the job. Being on salary, my "hourly" wage was incredibly small. There were usually a lot of stressful situations and of course, drama with teenagers. (*Honestly though, the teens caused me less frustration than some of the adults I had to deal with at times*).

During my time with TRIO I became very involved with ASPIRE, which is an association supporting TRIO programs. I previously mentioned the Council for Opportunity in Education. COE is supported by associations such as ASPIRE across the nation. These associations are made up of employees who work for TRIO programs (*COE*). There are six states within the regional association of ASPIRE. Each state has a Board of Directors, and the president of each state board is a member of the regional ASPIRE board.

I served on the Board of Directors in many capacities over my 12 years of service. For the State board I held the offices of Wyoming State Secretary, State President-Elect, State President (twice) and State Past President. On the Regional board I served as Regional Secretary for two 2-year terms.

I was in the middle of my second term as Wyoming State President when I made the decision to retire. I put a lot of years of service into ASPIRE and learned a lot. I got the opportunity to go to Washington DC three times over the years, and even made it to a national COE Annual Conference in Times Square of New York City once. They were all awesome learning experiences and I met many wonderful people who care deeply about student success.

ASPIRE holds state and regional conferences each year and I was fortunate enough to have many opportunities helping plan and organize them. My son Theo asked me once, if I could own my own business, what

it would be, and I told him it would be event planning. I love it and I think I am good at it!

College Trips

I traveled a lot while working with Upward Bound, doing college trips with students, and going to different trainings and conferences over the years. I was fortunate to be able to participate in professional development all over the country. I met many amazing people who work hard to support and assist students.

College trips were always fun and rewarding. Some of these students had never before experienced many of the things we did and places we visited. It was valuable for students to get a sampling of the different colleges and universities they had to choose from. The trips were educational, enlightening and exhausting!

After a busy day of travel, touring campuses and keeping track of students, I was usually skeptical about going to sleep for the night. As staff, we would do room checks a couple times in the evenings, ensuring that everyone was accounted for and discuss the next days' anticipated activities before allowing ourselves to finally relax and go to bed.

I remember one night when I was particularly tired. As I laid my weary head on the pillow with a deep sigh, I heard a knock at my hotel room door. I jumped out of bed and was greeted by two young girls; one with a fist full of blood! She had stuck her hand into her overnight bag and sliced her finger open on her razor. I called my co-worker (who should be a doctor) and she came and bandaged her up. We laugh about things like this, now. Fortunately, we didn't have many injuries on our trips.

We always included cultural experiences on these expeditions, too. One time we took the students to a concert by Black Violin, which was amazing. My favorite part was when another co-worker went to the band at the end of the concert asking if they would come meet our students. Their drummer came out to our bus to talk to them. We were all very excited as he shared his own educational journey and encouraged the students in completing theirs. It was very heartening and inspiring!

I love fish and am an avid aquarium fan. Whenever possible, I would

try to schedule a visit to a fish hatchery. They were always fascinating to me. There are many lakes and reservoirs in this part of the country that are kept stocked with fish by the Game & Fish Department. The U.S. Game & Fish and the U.S. Forest Service personnel were always happy to give personalized presentations to our students when we would come to their facilities.

Sometimes we rented a bus, but most times we rented several vans. I remember one time when we were headed to the vehicle and several students all yelled "shotgun" at the same time. I was then faced with deciding who would get the prized front passenger seat. Thinking fast, I held out an empty paper cup I had been holding and said, "here, throw this away" without looking at anyone. One young man grabbed it instantly and ran to the trash can with it. "You get shotgun!" I told him. Last time I saw that young man (he finished high school in 2012), he thanked me for all I had done to help him. These are just a few examples of my many experiences with students.

My students soon learned that riding shotgun meant two things. One; they had to stay awake and talk to me while I drove while other students slept in the back. Two; they got to play with the radio. They also knew that rap and country music were not allowed in my car! *Rock and roll, baby*!

I enjoy paperwork and there was always lots of it to do, but my favorite part of the job was working with students. More than once I told Dale that I was falling in love with a new group of students. Ideally, I would recruit them at the end of their eighth-grade year then work with them throughout high school until they graduated and went off to college. I loved being a mentor to students and got very close with many of them.

The most successful students were those who put the most effort into meeting with me to work on their various college readiness skills. By successful, I mean finding the best scholarships and getting accepted into the schools of their choice. It was especially rewarding to work hard with a student and to see them win an elite scholarship and/or full ride to college.

I remain in contact with many of my former students, and still have great visits with many of them. I am continually asked to be a reference. I cherish each and every one of them. In fact, since retiring, I recently saw one young gal I used to work with, and she told me she never appreciated how much I did for her and all the students until I was gone. That was a wonderful compliment coming from a 15-year-old girl!

I gained a lot of experience in this position. Besides working one-on-one with students, I gave many presentations, and worked with numerous schools and community partners. I met some of the most phenomenal people. I would list a few, but I don't want to risk leaving anyone out, so if you were one of my constituents, just assume that I am referring to you!

I put forth much effort into developing relationships with parents and family members of my students too, as I believe family support is extremely important when it comes to student success. I hosted family events at least three times per year. Funding was always an issue and I did spend a lot of my own money on the students, but I never regretted it. I thoroughly enjoyed planning events and college trips.

We had a director for many years who gave me much autonomy in my job and who allowed me the independence to do my own planning and preparation for the 3 to 5-day college trips. Sometimes we did trips with UB and UBMS students from the entire state, and sometimes I would plan trips with just my local students. We generally traveled out of state twice per year visiting several colleges and including cultural activities. We wanted students to get a feel for all the possibilities out there. It didn't matter where they attended college; we just wanted them to succeed in getting a bachelor's degree no matter where they chose to continue their education.

My Retirement

In 2018, I decided to retire. A change in supervisory staff brought about changes that I was not copacetic with. I won't go into detail (I did that in my exit interview) but the dynamics of my job changed significantly and I was no longer satisfied. I had become unhappy and frustrated and began praying for resolution. I started looking for another position, but when I realized I could retire early; that seemed to be the answer to my prayers. At this point in my life, it was imperative for me to surround myself with positivity and positive people. I realized that if I was unhappy it was up to me to change things.

Deciding to retire was not an easy decision to make, but once I made it, it felt so right! The most difficult part, of course, was leaving the students. I announced my planned departure in a group meeting as I spoke to the students about the different chapters in our lives.

"Why do you want to do well in high school?" I asked them. They responded with "to go to college." I then asked, "why do you want to go to college?" Their responses included "to get a job or career." We went on to discuss the different things we do in the varying stages of our lives until I asked, "and what do you expect to do at the end of your career?" They chimed, "retire!" "Yes!" I told them, "and that is what I am getting ready to do!"

There were mixed emotions, of course. There were a few tears, as they realized it meant I wouldn't be there the next school year, but for the most part, they understood. I gave a three month notice and tried to prepare them as best I could. I continued to work with them through the end of the semester, and we ended with a wonderful celebration.

For more than a decade, I had always planned a special end-of-the-school-year event for my students to celebrate and commemorate their accomplishments. This year, some of my friends and co-workers surprised me with a retirement party at the end of my annual student banquet. The best part is that besides my wonderful friends, community partners and co-workers, there were students, families and even former students all celebrating my retirement with me. I was brought to tears by the kind words that were spoken about me at the event. Especially those from my students. Thank you again to those of you reading this who participated!

I will note that, even though I gave a three-month advance notice of my retirement in March, 2018, my replacement wasn't hired until the end of the following October. My supervisors relied on temporary hires and employees of other TRIO programs and Gear Up (a sister college prep program) to help cover so students weren't abandoned.

I want to give a shout out to my wonderful friends from these programs for the help they gave students who were without a local project coordinator all those months. I worked with many amazing people over the years and I will never forget them!

My Health

As for my actual retirement; I am loving it! Although it brought a major change in how I deal with diabetes. Because of the change in insurance coverage, I had to go off the insulin pump. Supplies for my old pump had become difficult to find due to it being outdated. I did not have the financial means to purchase a new one.

Thanks to President Obama and the Affordable Care Act, I was able to find reasonable insurance. I have gone back to taking shots several times a day. I feel like a human pincushion, but I seem to be maintaining decent control of my blood sugars by checking my blood many times a day. Only another insulin dependent diabetic can appreciate the roller coaster ride involved in maintaining blood sugar control! Maybe when I become eligible for Medicare, I can afford to get back on the insulin pump.

I found a doctor I like, and other than enduring the symptoms of a Type 1 diabetic, I am extremely healthy. I am proud to say that the only medication I take is insulin. I can't say I never get sick, but I do strongly believe in the power of the mind when it comes to health. I take a vitamin every day (that I remember to), and I wash my hands whenever I use a public restroom to try and avoid contaminated germs. Whenever someone in the house gets a cold or sickness, I try to consume a lot of zinc and vitamin C, and I always drink lots of water.

Some may scoff at this, but whenever I do feel a sore throat or pain of some kind coming on, I do my best to resist it. I mentally "refuse" to accept any sickness without a mental battle. I meditate on healing and can feel a sort of "wave" going through my body as I mentally envision my blood cells fighting whatever is trying to make me sick. I make a point of never claiming ownership of sickness. For example; instead of saying "I have a cold" I will say "I'm fighting off a cold." For the most part, it works. I do try to eat healthy and take care of myself. *(I haven't figured out yet how to heal my pancreas but will let people know when I do)*!

CHAPTER 13

Luke's Return

I dreamt frequently of Luke throughout the years. I often visited with my little boy in my dreams. We would talk, laugh, and I would experience the tenderness and affection we shared. These realistic dreams helped me to cope with his loss. In the most recent dream that I remembered having about Luke; after hugging and chatting, my little boy walked out of the dream and a grown man walked into it. I was seeing Luke as a man.

While my heart still aches when I think of all the cherished moments over the years that I missed with my little boy, I always knew without a doubt, that I would see my son once again. I only realized during that dream that when I would at last see him again it would not be as my little boy; but as a grown man.

I grieved so much for Luke over the years that I actually got to the point where I felt like I ran out of tears. From the day I left my little son in Iran, I thought of and prayed for him daily. I always believed that God would reunite us someday. When I was going through the difficult phases of alcohol use and addiction, I know now that they were just feeble attempts to cover up the guilt, the painful memories, and the feelings of loss I had experienced regarding Luke.

I often think counseling back then would have given me much healthier coping skills than "numbing" myself the way I did, but finally getting into recovery saved my life. If I had not gotten clean and sober, learned so much about myself, and become a stronger, more capable and confident woman, I never would have been able to do the things I needed to do to help Luke eventually return.

I heard from Luke occasionally over the years. Luke told me that on his birthdays he always asked to call his mom. He didn't always get to, but each time that he was allowed to call we cherished our visits with each other. Of course, our conversations were monitored on his end, so we had to be careful about what we said. My parents always made sure to keep their phone number the same over the years, just in case Luke tried to call.

Luke told me that after his brief visit to the U.S. in the 1980's, when his dad whisked him away again, he wasn't allowed to contact me for many years. Once Luke turned eighteen, his uncle in Texas hired a private investigator and found my contact information. Luke made more than one attempt to reach me and when we finally spoke with each other again after ten years, it was very emotional. We began to communicate more often, but the messages weren't frequent because Luke had to use caution, since his father still monitored his emails. Luke eventually set up a secret email address and would email me from public cafenets, where internet was available. These emails set things in motion.

Shortly after the turn of the century, after spending several years studying Engineering, Luke was serving in the Revolutionary Guard Navy of Iran. Not by choice, but because Iranian men were not allowed to leave the country unless they had served two years in the military. Luke was treated very poorly while serving in their armed forces. Since he was tall, fair-skinned and born in America, he was considered a "westerner" and he was constantly accused of being a spy. One general often called him into his office to harshly interrogate and accuse him. Luke was fed up with his treatment there and had always longed to return to the United States and his mom.

He was prepared to attempt an escape from the torment and abuse he was experiencing, as well as all that he had endured most of his life growing up as an American in a country that abhorred "westerners." When he was finally able to ask for my help, I had to thank God I was clean and sober

and had my life and my mind in order. My emotional state when I was using left me unable to accomplish much of anything.

Luke told me his father refused to give him his American birth certificate, so I secretly mailed a copy to one of his friends, who then passed it along to Luke. His next step was to apply for an American passport. There was still no American Embassy in Iran, so he needed to go to the Swiss Embassy, who assisted Americans.

This was a difficult and lengthy process for Luke. Since he was serving in the Revolutionary Guard Navy, he had to bribe other soldiers to cover for him while he traveled over 15 hours one-way on an overcrowded bus to Tehron, the capitol of Iran. Once there, he had to battle their infamous city traffic. It took several more hours to get to the Swiss Embassy. More than once, he was late for his appointment due to traffic delays and was turned away. He would then have to wait another month for an appointment.

With much effort, I was able to contact the right person at the U.S. State Department and they contacted the Swiss Embassy in Iran. Eventually, the Swiss Embassy issued Luke a temporary American passport. Luke still had much to do in order to plan his escape from Iran.

The United States State Department put me in contact with the U.S. embassy in The United Arab Emirates (UAE) which lies across the Persian Gulf from Iran. I provided them with necessary information and purchased Luke an airline ticket to the United States. They then waited for Luke to arrive at their embassy. We didn't know exactly when that would be, but they were great people to work with. They would be ready for him.

It was the summer of 2003 when Luke finally began his trek across Iran to the Persian Gulf seeking a way out of the country. He had saved money over many years to be able to make the journey, and bribe those who might help him. He left with only the clothes on his back, his emergency U.S. passport, a small battery-operated fan, and the money he had saved.

He called me and told me it might be a few days before I heard from him again because he would have difficulty contacting me, but that the dangerous trek was finally beginning. We didn't know if he would be successful or not. If he were to be caught, he would surely be court martialed. Luke told me that desertion from the military and illegal emigration from the country are criminal offenses. Since he was legally an American citizen serving in their military, being caught meant he would be considered a spy and accused of treason. Treason is punishable by death in Iran. Luke said that any time an American was arrested, they were considered to be a spy. He knows of some Americans who still remain in Iranian prisons.

Needless to say, I was on pins and needles with fear and trepidation, as well as excitement and hopefulness. My family and I did a lot of praying during this time. I headed to Denver for an extended family get-together and began the wait. Several of my relatives from Colorado, Wyoming, Nebraska and California were all with me, waiting to hear any news.

I spoke daily with the U.S. embassy in the UAE who were also waiting to hear from him. There was an urgency on their part to get him to the airport as quickly as possible once he showed up at their embassy. An extradition treaty between Iran and the UAE would have to be adhered to by the embassy if Luke were caught. If Iran had requested his return, and the UAE officials knew he was in their country illegally, they would return him to Iran where he would have been imprisoned and severely punished. The U.S. embassy had to get him to the airport before any local officials knew he was there. Time was of the essence.

Meanwhile, Luke was in the midst of his dangerous excursion. As he traveled across Iran towards the Persian Gulf, he struggled to avoid authorities; not knowing if he had been reported missing. He found it difficult to trust anyone. Finding someone who would help him safely escape Iran was very risky. There were lots of people who would happily take his money, then report him to the police rather than help him.

For a price, he finally found people he felt he could trust who were willing to abet his escape and take him out to sea. He waited, hidden, for three days near the gulf before being taken to a fisherman's boat in the middle of the day, when most of the country are on their mid-day break. He was then borne far out into the ocean where he was put on yet another boat. This boat traveled to some sort of offshore platform where they waited for nightfall. Luke then boarded a small dinghy and he was placed in a hidden compartment in the hull of the boat with a bloke that Luke believes was a criminal escaping Iran. They were unable to converse since Luke spoke Farsi and English and the other man only spoke Arabic.

It was a miserable trip in that tiny boat heading into the Persian Gulf. The temperatures were as high as 120 degrees that day. The heat was nearly

unbearable on the tumultuous ocean in the tiny, cramped space. Luke's only relief was the small, battery operated fan that he'd had the foresight to bring with him.

They travelled nearly eight hours in this coffin-like compartment. The two stowaways were forced to bounce around in a space so tight they could barely move. At 6'6" Luke couldn't stretch his legs or even shift his position. He was crammed in with a stranger who barely spoke as they smelled each other's breath and soaked in each other's sweat. It was unquestionably a test of Luke's endurance as the boat slowly made its way across the Persian Gulf. The hope of seeing his mom again and of his future in America kept him going.

At one point, in my anxious state of waiting to hear from Luke, I was awakened by the shrill ring of my cell phone in the middle of the night. It jolted me from sleep and my heart raced as I reached for the phone; anticipating news of Luke's arrival to the UAE and the embassy. You can only imagine the despair I felt when that call turned out to be a drunk dialing the wrong number!

Once Luke finally arrived in the UAE, the first thing he did was buy a phone card. Although he was filthy, exhausted, and hungry, he told me of the relief he felt when he finally reached shore, called the embassy, and was told they had been waiting for his call. He had to find his way to the embassy, but once he got there, they were able to give him the documentation and paperwork he needed to start the last leg of his journey home. They swiftly escorted him to the airport where he boarded a plane to Germany with a layover there before heading to Denver, Colorado. An official from the embassy contacted me to let me know Luke was on his way at last!

It was a long flight for this exhausted young man, but such a relief for him to finally be on his way home. I was ecstatic! The miracle I had prayed for over the last 23 years was finally happening! My family was also excited, but most of the relatives at the reunion had to leave before he would arrive due to their own schedules. They were sad to be missing his arrival after waiting with me for so long but expressed much love and encouragement.

My beautiful cousin, who I share a birthday with, called a local news station in Denver before she returned to California, to see if they would be interested in the story. As my then eleven-year-old son Rocky and I waited in the airport, the media arrived with an anchor and cameraman. My dear former sponsor Spice came all the way from her hometown to share this wonderful event with me.

This last leg of anticipation seemed like it took forever. We had been waiting for what seemed like hours after Luke's plane had landed and other people had departed, but we still had not seen him. I finally went to someone at the international flight customs area and asked about Luke. They escorted me to a room in the back and began to question me extensively about Luke and the history of what had happened with him. Apparently, they had doubts and suspicions regarding this young man who had arrived without proper American identification and documentation. They asked me many questions before sending me back out to continue the wait.

I had so many different emotions going through my head. I never dreamed, after all his struggles to escape Iran, that he would have trouble getting through customs in the states. Was it possible they wouldn't release him? When they did, would I recognize him? Would he be happy to see me? What kind of a person would he be? Was I prepared to see, not the little boy I had longed for all those years, but a grown man who I knew very little about? My waiting was soon to end.

When the good-looking, yet extremely thin young man with light skin and dark hair finally exited the doors I had been watching, I knew him instantly! It was the young man I had seen in my dream!

The film crew captured our long overdue embrace on video and it was later shown on local news in Denver. We shared many tears of joy and relief! We were together again at last! Luke had never forgotten his mother who he knew loved him with all her heart. He was happy to meet his newest little brother, and we began the next chapter of our lives.

Luke had inherited his kind, loving nature from me. Our demeanors and nature are so much alike, we would be good subjects in a study for the nature vs. nurture debate. We spent the next few weeks getting to know each other better, and Luke often told me how wonderful it was to finally be able to relax. Life in Iran, for him, was full of fear and challenge. To say that life in the U.S. with his loving mother and family, was a relief, was a powerful understatement.

Here, Luke didn't look out of place, as he had his whole life in Iran. He

was much taller and fairer than most Iranians. He was (and still is) a tall, handsome, light skinned man with black hair and a warm, gentle smile. We loved getting to know each other again. It was a miracle and a dream come true for both of us!

On Luke's 26th birthday, not long after his return, I threw him a big birthday party. I gave him 24 gifts…one for his 26th birthday and one for each of the 23 birthdays I had missed with him. They weren't big expensive gifts, but there were so many things he needed, this was a fun way to provide them. It was a wonderful event! Mom cooked a delicious brisket with lots of side dishes, and we all feasted and rejoiced as many friends and family gathered to celebrate this special, joyous occasion!

Luke spent some time with me after his return and later with his brother Lyle in Ohio. He then joined his sister Bessie in Mississippi for a while. After a few months of searching for his calling and direction for his new life, Luke travelled to Texas to visit with his uncle. I prefer not to name the uncle, since it is risky for him. Luke tells me there is an Iranian cyber army who is continually looking for spies.

Once Luke arrived in Texas, he found a community of Iranians living in the United States. He made many new friends during the visit and soon decided to move there. While I was sad to see him move away from me permanently, I was also excited for the adventures he had in store there. He felt more American there than he had anywhere else. *Luke reports that the Texas city he now lives in is one of the most diverse cities in the United States with many opportunities and much potential.*

Luke worked hard doing various jobs. He usually held two or three different jobs at the same time. While working as a parking lot attendant, he met Shaquille O'Neill. The celebrity was always so pleased that he didn't have to readjust the seat after the 6'6" Luke brought his car back to him, that he always gave a very generous tip. After gaining experience in a large parking garage, Luke began his own valet parking service; working special events.

… *Alexandra Flowers*

Las Vegas Wedding

After settling in Texas, Luke met Lili, a wonderful young woman who shared a similar background. Lili's father is Iranian and her mother, who sadly died when she was very young, was American. She was born a citizen of the United States, but after her mother died, her father sent her to Iran to be raised by his parents. She returned to the United States as a young adult, with plans to attend college. Luke and Lili met, fell in love, and had a lovely wedding in Las Vegas.

Their Las Vegas wedding was only the second time in my life that all five of my children were together. The first time was shortly after Luke returned to the states. At that time, my kids all gathered and gifted me with a beautiful Mother's Ring they had made with the five gemstones representing each of my children.

Luke and Lili were married in February, and I decided to rent a 12-passenger van to drive to Vegas from Wyoming so we could all fit in one vehicle. Lyle and his wife had moved to our town for a while with their baby, Evie. We all loaded up in the van and proceeded to drive south during the winter. I will never do that again.

We experienced road closures due to wind and snow and took alternate routes after waiting on the highway for hours. What should have been a twelve to fifteen-hour drive took us almost three days. Let me tell you, driving on snow and ice is not fun, especially on mountain roads. At one point, in the middle of the night, we stopped at a gas station to rest and fill up before continuing the journey. As we were all heading inside, I started to slip on the ice-covered sidewalk. Lucky for me, when Beau hit the ice, he slid right into me and we kept each other from going down.

Lyle wasn't so lucky. He went down hard when he slid on the ice and broke his arm between the shoulder and elbow. What a nightmare! He ended up at the emergency room in a small Utah town. They wanted to keep him overnight, but Lyle was Luke's best man and he did not want to miss the wedding! The nearest town with an all-night drug store was almost 300 miles away, but Lyle wanted to tough it out. After waiting several hours at the hospital, we drove through the night and made it to the pharmacy to fill his prescription for pain medication before continuing

the journey. Lyle was suffering considerably, but we made it in time for a short rest before the wedding.

The wedding and reception were at Excalibur Hotel & Casino and were very nice. Luke had ordered a margarita bar, and a virgin margarita bar for the children and non-drinkers. We all had a great time, but at some point, Lyle was "accidentally" given a non-virgin drink. Considering his pain meds and state of exhaustion, we ended up having to put him in a wheelchair for the rest of the evening. We survived the trip, though and eventually made it home again with no more weather closures or injuries! Lyle had a long, rough recovery, though.

Luke and Lili are very happy together. I can see by the way Lili looks at Luke that she is very much in love with him. Within a couple years, they had a beautiful baby boy whom they named Leo. Leo is an extremely bright little boy who is fluent in both English and Farsi.

Luke's grandfather died a few years ago, but his grandmother in Iran is still alive. He would love to see her and other Iranian family again, but if Luke were to return to Iran, he would undoubtedly be arrested as a spy and prosecuted.

Today, Luke works long hours as Vice President and Asset Manager of a commercial real estate company and was recently highlighted in Redwood Media's Top 100 Magazine.

He hopes to write his own motivating story one day, with more details of his life in Iran, the loss of his mother, the abuse he endured at the hands of his father who had become an opium addict, and his eventual escape from Iran.

Luke wants people to know that no matter where they come from or what they have been through, with hard work and perseverance, they can succeed in life. He is proof!

CHAPTER 14

My Family Today

Being a workaholic, I hardly ever saw my kids and grandkids while I was working full-time. I now try to take every opportunity I can to go see them. I also have many cousins around the country whom I adore. On my mom's side, we try to have regular family reunions.

The family of my dad's generation has all passed away and I dearly miss them. I still talk to my cousins on my dad's side, but don't see them nearly often enough.

I send my love to my precious grandparents, aunts, uncles, and cousins who have left this world, and to the family members they left behind. They will never be forgotten.

Nothing makes me happier today than being with my kids, grandkids and family.

Bessie & Her Family

Bessie's son Beau has had his share of battling the demons of addiction. He was diagnosed with ADHD, ODD and several other emotional

disorders at a young age. He was always a very sweet, generous boy, but could never sit still. I can remember him climbing shelves before he could even walk!

Sadly, when he went to live with his mom again, after I graduated from college, they both ended up being horribly mistreated by Bessie's significant other; the same man Bessie was with when she took Beau back from me, who I had such a bad feeling about. Once I learned how grueling her situation was, I helped them escape, and they returned to my hometown.

Bessie's escape was similar to mine, although she was in Mississippi and not in another country. I bought plane tickets for Beau and her to return to Wyoming. She convinced her abusive, controlling partner that she needed to go to the department store to pick up school supplies for Beau. When he finally allowed her to leave the house, she went straight to the airport. She was terrified when she saw his aunt and uncle on her flight. She was worried that they would call their nephew to say they had seen her. Fortunately, she managed to avoid them.

He was outraged when he did discover what she had done and made many death threats to her and to our family. We managed to keep her safe though, and he finally relented and left her alone. (He probably found a new victim). It is ironic that she also ended up in an abusive relationship. She wants to write her own story as well.

Bessie proceeded to start her life anew and is a delightful, creative, wonderful young woman who now has an amazing life partner, Benny. He is a gifted bicycle mechanic, and he treats her with the love and respect she deserves. After spending time in Colorado and Ohio, Bessie and Benny are currently living in central Texas, where much of his family lives. Bessie has always been very caring and giving; always feeding the homeless and helping others any way she can.

When Beau was about 16, he brought home a 14-year-old homeless teen named Ray, whom he had befriended. Bessie took him in as her own and he stayed even after Beau left home. After searching for more than a year for this young man's father, it took Bessie less than 15 minutes to convince him to sign guardianship of Ray over to her. Bessie and Benny consider him as their son.

Ray's girlfriend, Hannah, also came to live with them after they moved

to Texas and she became a part of the family, as well. A couple years ago, they came to my town and I helped get them both into a program that facilitated them getting their General Education Diplomas. They lived with Dale and I for five months before they moved back to Ohio so that she could care for her ailing grandmother.

These two have had difficult lives, both having drug-addicted parents, but they turned out to be amazing young people. I miss them a lot and they call me Grandma. I love them dearly and I enjoy seeing them when I visit Ohio.

Beau had issues throughout his teen years with running away from uncomfortable confrontations, etc. He is very big-hearted and caring but was always a challenge. At one point, not long after he and Bessie returned from Mississippi, when he was in a recovery center, the depths of his stepdad's horrendous abuse came forward and he was diagnosed with PTSD. The abuse was reported to the state, but nothing ever happened.

This abuse explained much of Beau's behavior, but we never had the funds to truly get him the help he needed. His mom qualified for Medicaid but whenever he would go to a treatment center, they would only cover costs for a few weeks, which was never long enough to really help him with his mental health issues. Fortunately, he was never violent, but he had sticky fingers, couldn't be trusted, and frequently ran away. His involvement with drugs had him in and out of treatment centers and jail. He lived off and on in Ohio and Colorado over the next few years.

In 2015, he returned to my town and I helped him get enrolled in college. He tested extremely high on his entrance exams. Shortly after the semester started, he and his new girlfriend conceived a child and Beau dropped out of school to get a job. Sadly, they broke up before their baby boy was born.

Bessie and I have put effort into maintaining a relationship with the mama and do get to spend time with the little guy. He is an adorable baby and the spitting image of his daddy. She is a wonderful parent to him, and we very much appreciate her allowing us to be a part of his life. I am very proud of my great grandson's heritage. His mama is 100% Native American and his daddy is 25% Persian.

As of this writing, Beau is incarcerated in another state for drug related offenses and we have hopes of him turning his life around. Those who have

known and experienced addiction, understand how precarious recovery can be, but we love him and can only hope for the best. (*There is hope for all of us, right?*)

My Boys

Lyle works with computers and lives in Ohio with his partner Virginia. He shares custody of his wonderful daughters Evie and Trish with his first wife. They have been divorced a couple years now, but I will always think of her as my daughter-in-law and she is a wonderful mother to their girls.

Lyle found love again when he found Virginia. She is a truly amazing woman who works for a university in Cincinnati. With our shared love of students and education, we have much in common. They are planning to get married next summer. I consider her a dear friend and they are very happy to have found each other.

I love spending time with all of them and Lyle has told me I will always have a place to live with him. They always welcome me into their home and if it weren't for my attachments with Dale in Wyoming, I would go live with them in a heartbeat!

Theo and his wife own a successful business in South Carolina and have two adorable daughters. I just can't get enough of these precious little girls. I fell in love with the Charleston area when I first visited them there and look forward to returning. They are amazing parents and are both beautiful, talented, and caring people. While still in Colorado, Theo was selected as one of Northern Colorado's 40 under 40 Emerging Leaders and recently won a national award for franchisee of the year.

When they moved from Colorado to South Carolina it was a big leap of faith for them. Theo's neighbors found it amusing that Theo brought his snow shovel with him when he moved there. However, there was a surprise snowstorm in South Carolina a couple years ago. No one was laughing when Theo was the only person shoveling snow from the sidewalks!

There is an inexpensive flight between the two states where Lyle and Theo live, and I would be happy to spend all my time going back and forth between the two families! My favorite birthday ever was the first one after I retired. I got to have a birthday breakfast and lunch with my adorable little

granddaughters in South Carolina and a birthday dinner with Evie and Trish in Ohio! It is really important to me that my grandchildren know who I am, considering they all live so far away.

I was also able to reconnect with my charming cousin who lives in Charleston. I hadn't seen him in many years. He was very close to Papa growing up. His own father, who was married to Papa's older sister, died when my cousin was just a boy and Papa (his uncle) stepped up and mentored him. Not only is my cousin an amazing man, he looks a lot like Papa! I am very grateful to get to see him each year when I visit the area.

Today, **Rocky** has a double bachelor's degree, a loving girlfriend, and a good job. Rocky first met his sweetheart when he was elementary-school buddies with her big brother. They reconnected with each other years later. They both have good jobs in the same town I live in and are amazing young people. Rocky has considered graduate school but is currently working hard to pay off student loans, which built up despite his many scholarships. Since we live near each other, I am fortunate to get to see them more often than my other kids. Rocky has turned out to be a remarkable young man. I am so proud of him and who he has become.

Luke, Lili and Leo are still in Texas. Last time I went to visit, Bessie and her family, Luke and his family, and I all met up in Galveston and rented a beach house. I do love the beach. Our next planned visit is to meet in San Antonio.

A few years ago, four of my five kids made it to Las Vegas for Christmas. Unfortunately, Theo and his family couldn't make it on that trip. Last year, four of my five were able to spend a week together at Myrtle Beach in South Carolina. It was an amazing vacation. Sadly, Luke and his family were unable to join us on that excursion. At our most recent reunion, in 2019, only three of my five kid were able to attend.

Having all five of my kids together is far too rare for me, but it brings me the greatest joy. While I have seen all my kids and grandkids at different times, I look forward to the day we can all be together again when it is not for a funeral. The last time we were all together was in 2014, when Papa passed away. While we were all a huge comfort for each other, it was obviously a time of great sadness rather than joy. **Having all five of my children together again is at the very top of my bucket list!**

CHAPTER 15

The Last Of The Lions

As I began to accomplish goals in my life, such as getting clean and sober and going back to college, my sense of self-worth also grew. The lions surrounding my dreams became less and less frightening. As time passed, I would find myself moving closer and closer to those ferocious-looking lions. I would be dreaming about something entirely unrelated but would continually be aware of the lions bordering the dreams. By the time I graduated from the university and had many years of sobriety and success in my life, I was at the point where I was no longer a shy, insecure girl. I even got to where I enjoyed public speaking and in challenging myself to reach out and do more things.

I learned to be an advocate for myself.

Eventually, I reached the point where I casually walked right through the packs of lions in my dream; even petting them as I passed. I stopped, turned, and gazed back at them; realizing they weren't frightening at all. After all my years of dreaming about them and being so intimidated by them, I realized these same lions now just appeared to be big lazy cats.

> *That was the last time I dreamt of those lions. I had overcome my tremendous fear of them; just as I had overcome a magnitude of fear in my conscious life. This was very powerful for me in gaining a better understanding of how far I had evolved personally.*

I have taken the opportunity at this juncture in my life to write this long overdue book. I don't know if anyone will want to read it, but I needed to write it. In part, as a legacy for my children and theirs. One of the best things I heard from one of my grown sons once was when he told me that he felt he learned something from my mistakes. Most people need to go out and make their own. I used to say, "sometimes you have to find out who you're NOT in order to find out who you really are." I don't want my kids and grandkids to have to find out the hard way.

Often, when I am going through a difficult time, and cannot seem to stop my magical magnifying mind from over-thinking, I must force myself to STOP thinking. I repeat three words over and over to myself. These words are "strength," "wisdom," and "courage." I repeat, strength, wisdom, courage; strength, wisdom, courage; strength, wisdom, courage etc. until I achieve some speck of peace. It can even help me fall asleep at night when I can't seem to cease stressing or anticipating something. Just stopping my spiraling thoughts and attaining even a smidgen of serenity changes the course of my negative thinking.

I picked these three words loosely based on the Serenity Prayer written by Reinhold Niebuhr in 1934 (*Shapiro*). "*God, grant me the serenity to accept the things I cannot change; the courage to change the things I can; and the wisdom to know the difference*". If you really think about the meaning of these words, their sentiment is powerful.

The following is how these three words bring comfort to me:

"*Strength*" to get through whatever I am needing to get through by utilizing wisdom and having courage.

"*Wisdom*" to know what the next right thing to do is, as well as the wisdom to remember that I have gotten through difficulties in the past by applying strength and courage.

"*Courage*" to not give up; and to make it through. Nothing difficult

lasts forever; I will get to the other side of whatever my struggle is, provided I have strength and wisdom.

Pick your own mantra of words that help or have meaning for you. Remember that "different doesn't mean worse" and that you CAN make it through seemingly impossible trials as long as you don't give up. Have strength, wisdom, and courage.

In the future, I would love to travel and to share my experiences and victories with others; from the pain of losing Luke to the joy of being reunited with him; the experiences I had with refugees and teenagers; my huge accomplishments of getting and staying clean and sober for more than 20 years, fulfilling my life-long dream of returning to college; and even the amazing relationship I have with God today.

I implore you, dear readers, to overcome your own fears and fulfill your dreams. Surround yourself with positive people and discover what makes you happy. Learn how to feel and how to have fun without needing drugs, alcohol or other chemicals.

Be good to others and make the most of your lives. Based on my own experiences, whenever you are in a bad place, or having a difficult time, be sure to do something to help someone else. This always makes a positive difference; in your life as well as in theirs.

Just as it is difficult to find the "*manzana de agua*" fruit that I so dearly loved in Costa Rica, finding joy and happiness in life can be difficult and challenging; but oh, so worth it! Remember, that **happiness is a choice**! Whatever happens in my future, I plan to continue to work at finding joy in the next chapter of my life. My hope is that you, the readers of this book, can also appreciate my journey as you seek your own joy!

BIBLIOGRAPHY

About Ronald E. McNair, Ph.D.. Ed. np. nd. Web. 21 May 2019. <www.mcnairscholars.com>.

Alcoholics Anonymous, Home Page. *Home Page*. 2019. Web. 18 May 2019. <aa.org>.

COE. Ed. COE. nd. Web. 18 May 2019. <www.coenet.org>.

Foster Care. nd. web. 22 Mar 2019. <www.childrensrights.org>.

Heitz, David. *What Is Shyness?* 2013 13 Dec. np. web. 10 Mar 2019. <www.healthline.com>.

Home Page. 2019. Web. 16 May 2019. <www.cpiinflationcalculator.com>.

Iran Hostage Crisis. nd. np. Web. 16 May 2019. <www.u-s-history.com>.

Jenkins, Loren. *Panama's Banks Face Ruin*. 10 Apr 1988. np. web. 12 Mar 2019. <www.washingtonpost.com>.

Methamphetamine. nd. np. web. 16 May 2019. <www.drugabuse.gov/methamphetamine>.

Our Story. nd. np. Web. 18 May 2019. <www.matthewshepard.org>.

Shapiro, Fred R. *The Chronicle Review: Who Wrote the Serenity Prayer?* 28 Apr 2014. np. web. 16 May 2019. <www.chronicle.com>.

Made in the USA
Coppell, TX
01 January 2020

13978340R00099